PATHWAYS to REFORM

Remembering the Reformation after 500 Years

Benjamin Hawkins

Copyright © 2017 by Benjamin Hawkins. All rights reserved.

No part of this book may be reproduced, stored in a retrieval system, or transmitted by any means without the written permission of the author.

Unless otherwise indicated, Scripture quotations are from The ESV® Bible (The Holy Bible, English Standard Version®), copyright © 2001 by Crossway, a publishing ministry of Good News Publishers. Used by permission. All rights reserved.

Scripture quotations marked NASB are from the New American Standard Bible®, Copyright © 1960, 1962, 1963, 1968, 1971, 1972, 1973, 1975, 1977, 1995 by The Lockman Foundation. Used by permission. www.Lockman.org.

Scripture quotations marked NKJV are from the New King James Version®. Copyright © 1982 by Thomas Nelson. Used by permission. All rights reserved.

CONTENTS

Acknowledgements		7
Introduction		9
1.	'The word of our God will stand forever'	15
2.	'The end of the world was long ago'	19
3.	Roasted Goose and Singing Swan	23
4.	Renaissance and Reformation	27
5.	Luther's Declaration of Christian Liberty	31
6.	Luther's Reformation of Work and Rest	35
7.	'I Cannot, Will Not Recant'	39
8.	An Affair of Sausages, a Reformation Untamed	43
9.	'The Articles Wherefore John Frith Died'	47
10.	Live by the Sword, Die by the Sword	53
11.	'Truth is Immortal'	59
12.	Did Baptists Grow from Anabaptist Seed?	63
13.	A Ministry of Word and Spirit	67
14.	Calvin and the Calvinists	71
15.	Catholic Renewal and Reaction	75
16.	Roman Catholic Counter-Reformation	79
17.	Strange Bedfellows of the English Reformation	83
18.	'That We Finally Lose Not the Things Eternal'	89
19.	'Reformation Without Tarrying for Any'	95
20.	A Religion of the Book: The King James Bible	99
21.	Baptists, Pilgrims and the Cry for Freedom	103
22.	Revolution and the End of the Reformation Age	107
23.	'We are beggars! That is true!'	111
Notes		115
Further Reading		123

ACKNOWLEDGEMENTS

In this book, I've limited endnotes, as much as possible, to direct quotations or information that cannot be commonly found in histories of the Reformation. However, this book is the fruit of more than a decade of reading about the Reformation, and the "Further Reading" section at the end of the book suggests some of the sources that have been significant for me. Moreover, this book reflects the labor of those fantastic church historians who personally invested in me at Southwestern Baptist Theological Seminary in Fort Worth, Texas: John Mark Yeats (now at Midwestern Baptist Theological Seminary), Jason Lee (now at Cedarville University), Robert Caldwell, Dongsun Cho, the late Robert Bernard, and especially Malcolm B. Yarnell III, my doctoral supervisor. I'll be forever thankful for their investment. Needless to say, any faults in this book are not theirs, but my own. Additionally, I am grateful to *Pathway* editor Don Hinkle for allowing me to write this book and for supporting me so wholeheartedly. Above all, I want to thank my wife, Heather, and our children, Emma and Noah, for their support and love as I've studied and written about the Reformation during the past several years.

Benjamin Hawkins
July 1, 2017

INTRODUCTION

This book is first and foremost a resource intended for Missouri Southern Baptists, and it draws together a series of columns I wrote for *The Pathway*, the news journal of the Missouri Baptist Convention, during the year leading up to the 500th anniversary of the Reformation on Oct. 31, 2017.

During the 16th-century, men and women throughout Europe saw a need for reform in the church, and many of them tried to forge their own pathways for such reform. By no means can this book explore these pathways of Reformation history comprehensively or in great depth. Instead, it attempts to map out for you the pathways that the Reformers carved out as they tried to mend the church of their own day, and it brings you to the trailhead leading into each of these pathways. I provide resources for further study at the end of this book, and I hope that you see this book as a beginning—rather than an end—to your exploration of these Reformation pathways.

Before beginning your journey in earnest, however, it may be helpful to map out more broadly the various pathways carved onto the landscape of Reformation history.

Precursors to the Reformation

Various attempts at church reform occurred prior to Martin Luther's stand for biblical supremacy and justification by faith alone. The Reformation was also preceded and informed by various intellectual movements and technological advances of the late Middle Ages. These pre-cursors to the Reformation include:

- **Catholic reform efforts:** During the centuries preceding the Reformation, various popes, councils, monks and mystics tried to purify the Christian religion and clean up the abuses that they saw in the churches of their day.

- **The Premature Reformation:** During the 14th and 15th centuries, John Wyclif in England and later John Hus in Bohemia called for a more extreme reformation in ways that foreshadowed the work of Martin Luther and other 16th-century Reformers. Yet these movements had only limited success.

- **Renaissance humanism:** Although not in itself a "reform" movement, Renaissance humanism encouraged people to look back to the sources of Christianity, including Scripture and the early church fathers. The Christian humanism of the Reformation period shouldn't be mistaken for the secular or atheistic humanism of our own day.

- **The printing press:** Introduced into Europe by Johannes Gutenberg in the 15th century, the printing press would later allow Reformers to distribute their message broadly throughout Europe.

16th-Century Pathways to Reform

Far from being one monumental "Reformation," what happened during the 16th century is better described as a kaleidoscope of various "reformations" that interacted with one another. As mentioned earlier, the landscape of Reformation history was shaped by multiple pathways to reform:

- **Luther and the Lutheran tradition:** While Martin Luther influenced various "reformations" across Europe, he is particularly seen as the fountainhead of the Lutheran tradition. After his death, however, Luther's impact on confessional Lutheranism was shaped as the Reformer's followers debated various interpretations and applications of his teaching.

- **The Reformed tradition:** Being birthed in Switzerland and in cities along the Rhine river, the Reformed tradition developed slowly, becoming crystallized in debates of the 17th century. In the early years, churches within this tradition were led by a variety of men, such as Huldrych Zwingli, Martin Bucer, Johannes Oecolampadius and, most famously, John Calvin. This tradition stood apart from the Lutheran tradition especially because of two doctrinal questions: First, was Christ's body really present in the bread and wine taken at the Lord's Supper? Second, what was the relationship between God's law and the gospel?

- **The Radical Reformation:** This reformation tradition embraces a wide and diverse spectrum of people and teachings. It embraces Anabaptists, like Balthasar Hubmaier and Menno Simons (the namesake of today's Mennonites), who taught that churches are subject to the authority of Christ alone and that only adult disciples of Christ should be baptized. It includes revolutionaries like Thomas Muntzer, who tried to purge the church with violence. It also includes rationalists like Michael Servetus, who denied basic tenets of Christianity, such as the Trinity, as well as spiritualists like Sebastian Franck, who denied the existence of a true church on earth.

- **The English Reformation:** Informed by the other "reformations," the English Reformation had a unique political catalyst. In particular, in the 1530s, King Henry VIII broke away from the Roman church in order to get a new wife – a wife, he hoped, who would give him a male heir to the throne. During the 16th century, the fluctuations of the English Reformation would be defined by Henry VIII and his children: Edward VI, who died as a boy; Mary I, often called "Bloody Mary" for her persecution of Protestants; and Queen Elizabeth I. The later English Reformation produced Puritans, the Pilgrims, English Baptists and the King James Bible.

- **Catholic Renewal/Counter-Reformation:** Both before and after Martin Luther's break from the Roman church, various Roman Catholic leaders and groups tried to reform church doctrine and practice. Some of these Catholic Reformers even endorsed views of justification similar to Luther's. But the Catholic/Counter-Reformation became crystalized in the mid-16th century at the Council of Trent, which rejected the teachings of Luther and other Protestant Reformers.

When did the 'Reformation' occur?

While modern Protestants celebrate the beginning of the Reformation on Oct. 31 each year, this date is merely a formal anniversary of the Reformation rather than the actual date of its beginning. Historians haven't agreed on any precise date for the beginning of the Reformation, partially because—as noted above—the "Reformation" was actually the collision of several "reformations."

Nor is the end of the Reformation easy to determine precisely. Many historians today see the Reformation as a long process rather than a single event. As such, one history of Reformation England begins in 1480 and ends in 1642.

Thus, while Oct. 31st marks a key moment at the beginning of the Reformation period, one should regard the "Reformation" as a collision of various "reform" movements—or a tangle of paths toward reform—that emerged and developed over a long period of time, especially during the 16th and early 17th centuries.

> "Christians should be exhorted to be diligent in following Christ, their head, through penalties, death and hell; and thus be confident of entering into heaven through many tribulations rather than through the false security of peace."
>
> -Martin Luther

1.

'THE WORD OF OUR GOD WILL STAND FOREVER'

Had he used a hammer, one could perhaps say that its sound would reverberate across Europe and, eventually, across the globe.

But contrary to legend, Martin Luther may have carried no hammer when, on Oct. 31, 1517, he approached the Castle Church in the small university town of Wittenberg, Germany, where he served as both priest and professor. Perhaps using paste instead of nails, he posted a set of 95 Theses for public debate on the church door, which served at the time as a community-wide bulletin board.[1]

Earlier that fall, Luther had introduced 97 different theses to faculty members at the university, and he was met then with some lively discussion from interested scholars and, no doubt, yawns from the others. But not so with his 95 Theses of Oct. 31st. Soon, these declarations from Luther's pen would go to print not only in Latin, the professional language of churchmen and academics, but also in the languages of the common folk—with drastic, and sometimes revolutionary, results.

These pungent theses criticized abuses of church power—especially the pope's attempt to raise funds for renovating St. Peter's Basilica in Rome by guaranteeing salvation to all who would simply donate to the building project. "As soon as the coin in the coffer rings, the soul from purgatory springs," Johann Tetzel, a famed seller of the pope's salvific guarantees (called "indulgences"), preached as he made his rounds throughout Germany.

In the 95 Theses, Luther decried such cheapening of God's grace, which distorted and watered down the message of salvation merely to collect cash. Instead, he insisted that the Christian life should be filled with repentance and that the "true treasure of the church is the most holy gospel of the glory and grace of God."

"Christians," he wrote in his final two theses, "should be exhorted to be diligent in following Christ, their head, through penalties, death and hell; and thus be confident of entering into heaven through many tribulations rather than through the false security of peace."[2]

Yet, when Luther fastened this message to the Wittenberg church door in 1517, there was no hammer. No nails. No resounding clang or thud. But we have to admit—Luther's glue worked well. After all, his message has stuck with us for centuries.

In fact, Christians across the globe celebrate the 500th anniversary of the Reformation that Luther started on Oct. 31, 2017. But, perhaps for many Christians, the question remains, "Why?" What is this Reformation? Why does it matter for people living in the 21st century? What should we make of it? And, most importantly, what did God have to do with it?

Of course, no one can sufficiently answer these questions without delving into the complexities of history, searching out the story of the Reformation for oneself. Nevertheless, the following chapters will present in summary fashion this story. But as Baptist church historian A.H. Newman wrote more than a century ago, any attempt to describe the workings of God during the Reformation defies simple explanation.[3]

"And here we must remember," Newman writes, "that the cause of God on earth progresses not in straight lines like a railroad train across yonder prairie, but like yonder tossing ship on yonder surging ocean." Likewise, any serious investigation into the lives and doctrines of the Reformers—men like Martin Luther, Martin Bucer, Huldrych Zwingli or John Calvin—should at least cure Baptists of "blind hero-worship." After all, as Newman writes, these very same Reformers, who proclaimed Christian liberty, "would not have hesitated to urge our extermination by fire, sword, or water, if we had been their contemporaries"—simply because we deny infant baptism and teach that water baptism should not precede a profession of faith.

Here we must remember that God often works through us in spite of ourselves. Newman reminds us that, "owing to the perversity of men," God's cause does not make "clear and constant progress," although it indeed progresses. "Sometimes it seems to lose ground; but, after all, the apparent loss is transmuted by divine alchemy into means of future gain." And this should be an encouragement for us, as we maneuver the difficulties of our own age.

Luther himself, who tended to see human efforts not only as vain but also often as a joke, recognized that God alone could advance his cause. For this reason, he once quipped that he had done nothing at all to make his Reformation succeed.

"I simply taught, preached, and wrote God's Word; otherwise I did nothing," he said. "And then, while I slept, or drank Wittenberg beer with my Philip and my Amsdorf, the Word so greatly weakened the papacy that never a prince or emperor did such damage to it. I did nothing. The Word did it all."[4]

And, perhaps, this is ultimately why we should celebrate Luther and the rest of the Reformers. For they trusted Scripture to make an impact in their age; despite numerous obstacles, they endeavored to publish it widely both in print and proclamation. And, without hammer or nails or glue, God's Word has stuck with us for centuries, resounding across the globe. Such was the core truth of the 16th-century Reformation, and such should be the crux of all our endeavors: "The grass withers, the flower fades, but the word of our God will stand forever" (Isaiah 40:8, ESV).

2.
'THE END OF THE WORLD WAS LONG AGO'

*"For the end of the world was long ago,
When ends of the world waxed free ...."*

– **G.K. Chesterton, The Ballad of the White Horse**[1]

"On a sultry day in July of the year 1505 a lonely traveler was trudging over a parched road on the outskirts of the Saxon village of Stotternheim. He was a young man, short but sturdy, and wore the dress of a university student. As he approached the village, the sky became overcast. Suddenly there was a shower, then a crashing storm. A bolt of lightning rived the gloom and knocked the man to the ground. Struggling to rise, he cried in terror, 'St. Anne, help me! I will become a monk.'

"The man who thus called upon a saint was later to repudiate the cult of the saints. He who vowed to become a monk was later to renounce monasticism. A loyal son of the Catholic Church, he was later to shatter the structure of medieval Catholicism. A devoted servant of the pope, he was later to identify the popes with Antichrist. For this young man was Martin Luther."[2]

With these words, Reformation historian Roland Bainton began his classic biography, *Here I Stand: A Life of Martin Luther*. As Bainton recounts, Luther's encounter with a thunderbolt sent the young man to the monastery. But why? After all, we wouldn't imagine that, in the same scenario, a 21st-century secularist from New York would respond as the young Luther had.

Luther's response to the thunderbolt was telling. It revealed his beliefs and deepest fears. For, as Bainton himself says, Luther was a medieval man. His parents taught him early in life to fear devils in the outhouse and—due to vestiges of German paganism in their thought—to fear elves, sprites and witches in the woods. More than anything, however, he feared the imminent day of doom at the end of the world, when the Lord Jesus Christ in majesty would judge the quick and the dead.

"It is not just the old Luther who sees the world coming to an end; already the young Luther has seen that the world has grown old," another famed Reformation historian, Heiko Oberman, writes. Like many medieval men and women, Luther did not see himself as living in a Middle Age. Rather, he saw himself as living at the end of all ages.[3]

Indeed, the idea that the Middle Ages was, well, "somewhere in the middle" was not the typical assumption of medieval men and women. Instead, this idea derived from people who saw themselves as having recovered a glorious past that had for some time been lost: According to the champions of the Renaissance and Enlightenment, the grand knowledge and artistry of ancient Greece and Rome had finally been reborn after being wrapped in barbarian darkness for a thousand years; according to heirs of the Reformation, the purity of early Christianity had finally been rediscovered and the gospel had dawned after a dark age.

But more recent thinkers have questioned this view of the Middle Ages. In fact, while speaking at his 1954 inaugural lecture as the Chair of Medieval and Renaissance Studies at Cambridge University, the renowned Christian author C.S. Lewis denounced the claim that Modern man had "scrambled ashore out of the great, dark surging sea of the Middle Ages."[4]

And, in a sense, he was right. The Middle Ages wasn't as "in the middle" or as "dark" as we often take it to be. After all, this time period—which runs roughly from 500 A.D. to 1500 A.D.—has given us much to be thankful for: For example, books replaced scrolls; universities were founded; biblical concordances were invented; scholars first formulated arguments for God's existence that are still used today by men and women defending Christianity. And, of course, the Middle Ages gave us Martin Luther. For, had not a thunderbolt knocked him into the monastery, he never would have broken out of monasticism to become a Reformer.[5]

But, of course, this begs the question: If the Middle Ages was so great, why all Luther's fuss about Reformation? Here again, we find roots in the Middle Ages for the very idea of "Reformation." After all, however wrong-headed they were, monasteries were started to preserve a purer devotion to Christ and his commands. And even various medieval popes and councils called for the church to be reformed in both root and branch. This is no wonder, since—during the 1300s—two and then three competing popes had at one and the same time claimed sole authority over the church in Western Europe.

Something was definitely amiss. Even if the Middle Ages weren't as dark as we often imagine, the medieval church had serious problems—and no one doubted it. But looking at the problems through the lens of his own study of Scripture, Luther would say that monastic and other medieval reform efforts had missed the mark. He insisted that no moral stricture, no pious effort, no institutional renovation would fix these issues. Medieval men and women, like those in our own age, must rather return to the truth of the gospel—namely, that Christ is all in all, and he is found and grasped by faith alone.

Now, there was a medieval cry for reform that, in some ways, foreshadowed Luther's own call for Reformation. Indeed, it presaged, if not the end of all ages, at least the end of the world as the young man Luther and his contemporaries had known it. It is this "morning star" of the Protestant Reformation that we'll consider in the next chapter.

3

ROASTED GOOSE AND SINGING SWAN

> *"…. The bishop gathered what he could.
> Beside the River Swift, he lit a pile of wood
> and tossed the bones on one at a time,
> cursing the heretic from limb to limb.
> Afterwards, they shoveled ash into the water
> and no one even thought the word martyr."*
>
> – Poet Thom Satterlee, "Burning Wyclif"[1]

In the summer of 1519, nearly 15 years after a thunderbolt had knocked him into the monastery and nearly two years after he publicly criticized the pope in his *95 Theses*, Martin Luther stood on a platform in Leipzig, Germany, defending his controversial ideas. His opponent in the dispute was Johann Eck, considered one of the fiercest debaters in the land. Although he met his match in Luther, Eck soon pinned him as a heretic in a way that even he didn't expect.

"I see," Eck said to Luther, "that you are following the damned and pestiferous errors of John Wyclif, who said, 'It is not necessary for salvation to believe that the Roman Church is above all others.' And you are espousing the pestilent errors of

John Hus, who claimed that Peter neither was nor is the head of the Holy Catholic Church."[2]

At first, Luther himself spurned the accusation that he was spreading other men's heretical ideas. He had no particular expertise in the ideas of Wyclif or Hus. Yet, after an evening of research, he returned to the debate with a startling admission.

"Among the articles of John Hus, I find many which are plainly Christian and evangelical, which the universal Church cannot condemn," Luther said.[3]

Nearly a century before Luther made this declaration, a council of church leaders meeting in the city of Constance, in southern Germany, condemned Hus as a heretic. They consigned him to be burned at the stake—despite the promise of a safe conduct to and from the council. A decade later, in 1427, the pope also commanded that Wyclif's corpse, which had been in the grave for 43 years, should be exhumed and burned.

This account raises two questions: Why were these men condemned as heretics? And what kind of legacy did they leave for Luther and other Reformers to build upon?

Born in the county of York, England, around the year 1328, Wyclif studied at the University of Oxford, where he was distinguished as a doctor in theology. Coming into the service of the king, he found the support of Duke John of Gaunt, himself a king's son, who protected Wyclif as he broadcast his radical ideas for reform. Among other ideas, he insisted that Scripture should be the supreme authority for the church's teachings. He also argued for the closure of monasteries and branded the pope as the Antichrist. Additionally, he attacked transubstantiation—that is, the belief that the bread and wine used during the Lord's Supper are miraculously transformed into the real body and blood of Christ. But despite his contentious ideas, and partially due to the protection he gained from John of Gaunt, Wyclif's life came to a natural and non-violent end in 1384.

But Wyclif's ideas didn't die. In England, they were spread abroad among a network of his followers, called the Lollards. Yet, after a failed attempt to grab political power for the movement, the Lollards were quickly pushed underground, where they fed on the English Bible translations inspired by Wyclif.

Wyclif's writings and ideas, however, also spread across the English Channel to the land of Bohemia, which bordered Eastern Germany. There, they found a strong proponent in Hus, who reshaped them and used them to promote his own vision for reform. Unlike Wyclif, Hus met a brutal end in 1415, yet his ideas also continued to flourish in Bohemia. Long before Luther faced accusations of heresy during the Leipzig debate of 1519, the Bohemians had broken away from Rome to create their own church based on the ideas of Hus.

No doubt, Luther promoted ideas similar to those of Wyclif and Hus. But when condemned as a Hussite during his Leipzig debate with Johann Eck, he immediately rebuffed the accusation. Despite similarities, Luther's vision for Reformation was fundamentally different than the visions of Wyclif and Hus, according to historian Heiko Oberman in his biography, *Luther: Man between God and the Devil*. Ultimately, Luther's roots as a Reformer didn't grow from the seed that Wyclif and Hus had sown.[4]

Nevertheless, as another historian has noted, Wyclif and Hus provided a fine "pedigree" for Luther and other Reformers, who needed support in their attack of the Roman church. English Reformer John Bale, followed by the more renowned John Foxe, later called Wyclif the "morning star" of the Reformation.[5] And Luther himself couldn't help but gain inspiration from Hus, the martyr.

"For Luther St. Hus-the-martyr was very much alive," Oberman writes in his biography. "Luther was convinced that the prophecy Hus had made before his execution applied to the Reformation: 'Holy Johannes Hus prophesied about me when he wrote from his Bohemian prison that they might now be roasting a goose ..., but in a hundred years they will hear a swan sing, which they will not be able to silence.'"[6]

And, indeed, even 500 years later Luther's swan-song continues.

4.
RENAISSANCE AND REFORMATION

Less famous than the Sistine Chapel, St. Peter's Basilica in Rome owes at least some of its brilliance to the same man: Renaissance artist Michelangelo Buonarroti.

Through windows at its base, light pours into the dome of St. Peter's from every direction, bringing to life its manifold frescoes and its gold and blue rays, which lead the eye upward to heaven. Below the windows, written in Latin with blue letters painted on gold, are words from Matthew 16:18-19: "You are Peter and upon this rock I will build my church, ... and I will give you the keys to the kingdom of heaven."

Of course, these words sit at the base not only of the dome at St. Peter's Basilica, but also at the foundation of the medieval papacy's claim to authority over the church. During the 16th-century Reformation, Martin Luther and other Reformers ousted the Pope's claim to power, pointing instead to faith in Christ as the church's one foundation.

In 1505, the "Warrior Pope" Julius II—one of Michelangelo's sponsors, for whose tomb the artist crafted his famous sculpture of Moses—decided to demolish the original basilica and replace it with architecture of the grand Renaissance style. Attempts to raise funds for the construction of this new basilica would, in 1517, ignite the Reformation by provoking Luther to pen his *95 Theses*. Regardless, the Renaissance Popes trudged forward with construction of the new building. And although Michelangelo didn't get to see the project completed before his death in 1564, his genius as an architectural designer can be viewed today by visitors to the site.

The fact that Michelangelo played a large part in the design of St. Peter's Basilica—a building project, as noted above, criticized by Luther himself—fits well into one common theory about the relation between Renaissance and Reformation. This theory was popularized among evangelical Christians by Francis Schaeffer in his book, *How Should We Then Live?* Not without reason, Schaeffer claimed that the Renaissance stood in opposition to the Reformation, the former centered on man and the latter centered upon God as revealed through His Word.[1]

However, as correctly argued by James R. Payton, Jr., in his book, *Getting the Reformation Wrong*, this view misinterprets the relation between Renaissance and Reformation.[2] Seeing these two movements in simple opposition is, well, too simple. In fact, the Renaissance—a roughly 13th-to 17th-century rebirth of art and learning, which drew especially from the well of ancient Greece and Rome—often fed into the Reformation. For example, during the same period that Michelangelo supported the papal church with his artistic talents, the German Renaissance artist Lucas Cranach the Elder became a mentor and friend to Luther—a relationship described in historian Steven Ozment's book, *The Serpent and the Lamb*.[3]

But the Renaissance wasn't restricted to the visual arts. Renaissance humanists—not to be mistaken for the secular, atheistic humanists we meet today—made advances in the study of language, literature and history. Of course, staunch Catholics were among humanist ranks. But these advances in the humanities also impacted many Reformers, and humanism sometimes provided them with tools for challenging the papal church. For example, defenders of the Pope's authority over Western Europe had often pointed to a supposedly ancient document, "The Donation of Constantine," in support of their cause, but the humanist Lorenzo Valla correctly exposed the document as a forgery.

One Renaissance humanist, in particular, had a significant—though ambiguous—relationship with the Reformation. That humanist was Desiderius Erasmus of Rotterdam. A Dutchman born in 1466, Erasmus attacked meaningless ceremonies and the abuses of the late medieval church—sometimes satirically, as in his work, *The Praise of Folly*. But he also called people to sincere and personal faith, and enjoined a widespread knowledge of Scripture. In an age when most Bibles were in Latin, a language that few people understood, Erasmus encouraged biblical translation from the original languages. He applied the humanist cry, "*ad fontes*," to the faith—that is, people should return to the Bible, "to the wellspring" of Christianity.

"Would that, as a result, the farmer sing some portions of [the Scriptures] at the plow, the weaver hum some parts of them to the movement of his shuttle, the traveler lighten the weariness of the journey with stories of this kind! Let all the conversations of every Christian be drawn from this source," Erasmus wrote in the preface to his own new Latin translation of the Greek New Testament, published in 1516.[4]

Erasmus' translation, which was printed side-by-side with the Greek original, would be used by many Reformers to translate Scripture. In fact, inspired by Erasmus' work, the English Reformer William Tyndale later proclaimed that, God-willing, he would see an English ploughboy learn more of Scripture than the average priest. And, using Erasmus' New Testament, Tyndale soon afterward published a translation that has shaped English renderings of the New Testament up to the present day.

It is ironic, therefore, that Erasmus never became a Protestant Reformer himself, but remained a faithful supporter of the Roman church until his death in 1536. Yet, especially through his biblical scholarship, his efforts as a Renaissance humanist left an indelible impact on the Reformation—and, as a result, on our lives today.

5.
LUTHER'S DECLARATION OF CHRISTIAN LIBERTY

In 1505, the young man Martin Luther, cowering before a thunderbolt, vowed to become a monk and a devout servant of the Catholic church under the headship of the Roman pontiff. Fifteen years later, in the summer of 1520, Pope Leo X launched his own thunderbolt at Luther in the form of an edict that denounced Luther as a "wild boar" destroying God's "vineyard," the Catholic church. The pope warned Luther to recant his errors within 60 days, lest he be condemned as a heretic and turned over to secular authorities for punishment.[1]

Why did Luther receive such a threat from the pope? As described in a previous column, Luther wrote *95 Theses* in 1517 that challenged the pope's authority and criticized the church's practice of raising income by guaranteeing people's salvation at a price. But by the time Pope Leo X published his edict (called a "papal bull"), it had become clear that Luther's dissent from the Roman church ran much deeper even than this.

Now, Luther didn't cower beneath the thunderbolt of the pope's edict. When he finally received the edict in the winter of 1520, he burned it alongside copies of Roman ecclesiastical law and books supporting the pope. Meanwhile, he had begun to write a series of three classic works outlining the fundamental nature of his call for reform. In the last of these brief treatises, called *On Christian Liberty*, Luther declared the foundation of his teaching: namely, that people can be righteous in God's sight by faith alone, and not by their own efforts.

For many years, Luther had himself been terrified by the righteous God who could justly condemn sinners to hell. However, sometime between 1514 and 1518, he gradually overcame his "hatred" for God's righteousness as he poured over various passages of Scripture—particularly, Romans 1:17, which reads, "For in [the gospel] the righteousness of God is revealed from faith for faith, as it is written, 'The righteous shall live by faith.'"[2]

Luther had previously struggled with Romans 1:17 because he thought the phrase, "the righteousness of God," referred to the righteous standard by which God judges sinful human beings. He wondered how such righteousness, supposedly revealed in the gospel, could be good news to helpless sinners. If this is what Paul meant by "the righteousness of God," does the gospel not offer fear of judgment rather than hope for mercy? Decades later, long after his battle with the Roman church had begun, Luther recounted how his understanding of God's righteousness changed:

> *"At last, by the mercy of God, meditating day and night, I gave heed to the context of the words [of Romans 1:17] .... There I began to understand that the righteousness of God is that by which the righteous lives by a gift of God, namely by faith. And this is the meaning: The righteousness of God is revealed by the gospel, namely, the passive righteousness*

with which the merciful God justifies us by faith, as it is written, 'He who through faith is righteous shall live.' Here I felt that I was altogether born again and had entered paradise itself through open gates."

In late 1520, standing firm against the pope's threats, Luther succinctly and profoundly defended this belief in *On Christian Liberty*. He explained that, for our spiritual health, life and righteousness, we need nothing but the Word of God—that is, in this instance, the gospel of Jesus Christ. And nothing can grasp the Word of God except faith alone. Good works cannot help us spiritually, nor can physical affliction harm us spiritually. In contrast, faith in the gospel brings righteousness apart from our efforts, and faith alone honors God, who promises salvation in the gospel.

By faith, Luther writes, our souls are united "with Christ as a bride is united with her bridegroom." Just as husband and wife share all things, even so Christ takes ownership of everything that belongs to us—including our "sins, death and damnation." Likewise, by faith, we receive from Christ everything that belongs to Him—including life, salvation and righteousness.[4]

Because we are united with Christ in faith, moreover, each of us is "a perfectly free lord of all, subject to none." We are completely free from slavery under sin or the law, and all things "work together"—as the apostle Paul writes in Romans 8—to bring about life, peace and salvation for us. At the same time, by faith in Christ, we are "priests," graciously empowered to approach God's throne and to pray for and teach each other. Such is the Christian liberty that we receive by faith.[5]

In contrast, Luther adds, each of us is a "perfectly dutiful servant of all, subject to all." Nevertheless, we don't serve anyone because we think that we can earn our way to heaven by our own efforts. Instead, we serve our neighbors out of the love poured into our hearts by God's Spirit. Faith in Christ doesn't free us to live in "idleness or wickedness"; rather, it frees us truly to love others, as Christ loves us.[6]

"We conclude, therefore, that a Christian lives not in himself, but in Christ and his neighbor. Otherwise he is not a Christian," Luther writes. "He lives in Christ through faith, in his neighbor through love. By faith he is caught up beyond himself into God. By love he descends beneath himself into his neighbor."[7]

Luther's declaration of Christian liberty was revolutionary, dismantling a late medieval religion consisting largely in attempts to earn one's way to heaven through good works. But in 1520 he could hardly have imagined the revolution that would soon sweep across Europe because of his message.

6.

LUTHER'S REFORMATION OF WORK AND REST

When Martin Luther proclaimed the truth that God justifies sinners by faith alone, he declared also that Christians must follow Jesus amid the joys and storms of day-to-day life in the world. There was no place, any longer, for secluding oneself to seek a holy life in a cloister. Whereas medieval religion placed monastic solitude and celibacy on a spiritual pedestal, Luther instead affirmed that God had ordained marriage, family and one's daily work as the altar where each Christian dies to himself, and as the classroom where he learns truly how to love God and one's neighbor. Whether ruling an empire, plowing fields or rearing children, each Christian's daily labor is an opportunity to trust God and imitate Christ's love by serving others.

In short, Luther's Reformation had an impact not only on religion, but also on work.

"I advise no one to enter any religious order or the priesthood," Luther wrote in 1520, in a brief tract called *The Babylonian*

Captivity of the Church. "Indeed, I advise everyone against it—unless he is forearmed with this knowledge and understands that the works of monks and priests, however holy and arduous they may be, do not differ one whit in the sight of God from the works of the rustic laborer in the field or the woman going about her household tasks, but that all works are measured before God by faith alone."[1]

Indeed, according to Luther, all works are measured by God—and, in themselves, they are found wanting. As the Prophet declared in Isaiah 64:6 (NASB), "all our righteous deeds are like a filthy garment," and as the Teacher says in Ecclesiastes 2:26 our labor and toil "under the sun" are all in vain, merely "a striving after the wind." Through the fall of the first man, Adam, all of us have died in sin and are unable to please God. Likewise, as God told Adam in Genesis 3:17, "Cursed is the ground because of you; in pain you shall eat of it all the days of your life; thorns and thistles it shall bring forth for you." As a result of the fall, our daily labor in this world became toilsome and often futile.

In short, sin tarnishes and enslaves our hearts and minds, and it brings the works of our hands to nothing.

And this is why Luther's message is such an encouragement: He declared that the sacrifice of Jesus Christ on the cross delivers sinful humanity from every effect of the fall. And to gain Christ, with all his benefits, we need only trust Him.

Only Jesus can cleanse our hearts and free us from sinful thoughts. So we must come to Him in faith. By faith alone, we are justified and made righteous in God's sight.

Likewise, only Christ's blessing can fill our daily work with true meaning and purpose. "Unless the Lord builds the house," the Psalmist says, "they labor in vain that build it. Unless the Lord guards the city, the watchman stays awake in vain" (Psalm 127:1, NKJV). In other words, we may plant a seed and water it, but only God can make it grow. We must, therefore, trust Him to do so in His time and in His way. We must trust Him to bring meaningful, eternal fruit from our daily labor. By faith in Christ Jesus, God is our Father. We are His children, and it is His "good pleasure" not only to care for our daily needs, but also to grant us a heavenly kingdom. As such, we should fear neither famine nor futility (Luke 12:32).

In this faith, we can find true security, peace and rest—knowing that our gracious Father can make our vocations, our relationships and our lives fruitful for His kingdom by faith in Christ. For this reason, Luther once commented to a close friend, "We worship God also when we rest; indeed, there is no greater worship of God than this."[2]

Explaining this comment in his book, *The Ethics of Martin Luther*, historian Paul Althaus once wrote, "How is it possible for us to worship God more when we rest than when we work? At this point we once again stand at the center of Luther's theology: God is God and he alone is creator. We can worship God by resting; indeed, in resting we can worship Him better than in any other way because it is when we really relax our body and soul that we cast our care on God. We thus honor God as the one whose blessing rests upon and surrounds all our work, and who keeps on working for us even when we rest and sleep. The capacity truly to rest from our cares with our body and soul is a special confirmation of our faith and is related to justifying faith."[3]

Or, as the Psalmist also says, "It is vain for you to rise up early, to sit up late, to eat the bread of sorrows; for He gives His beloved sleep" (Psalm 127:2, NKJV).

"

"Unless I am convicted by Scripture and plain reason, I do not accept the authority of the popes and councils, for they have contradicted each other. My conscience is captive to the Word of God. I cannot and will not recant anything."

-Martin Luther

7.

'I CANNOT, WILL NOT RECANT'

Martin Luther never planned to tear the medieval church apart. The division of western Christianity into its various denominations—Roman Catholic, Lutheran, Presbyterian, Anglican, Baptist, Mennonite—wasn't inevitable. Luther's declaration that sinners are justified—made righteous in God's sight—solely by faith in the death and resurrection of Jesus Christ didn't necessarily have to stir up the religious revolution that occurred in the 16th century.

Indeed, some theologians who ultimately sided with the Pope against Luther basically agreed with what Luther was saying about justification by faith alone. For example, Gasparo Contarini—a Cardinal in the Roman church—understood Luther's message about God's gracious gift of salvation and devoted much of his career (in vain) to helping reunify the divided church. When Contarini wrote his own tract on justification by faith, Cardinal Reginald Pole—who would oversee the brief restoration of Roman Catholicism in England during the mid-1500s—applauded him for shedding light upon "that holy, fruitful, indispensable truth."[1] Although sympathy for Luther's views about salvation would eventually be pushed out of the Roman church, these views weren't shunned by all Catholic churchmen when Luther first expressed them.

In that case, what about Luther's message was so revolutionary that it led to the break-up of the medieval church in Western Europe? A short essay can't answer this question fully, but here is a brief response: Prodded along by circumstances and by his enemies' rebuttals, Luther ultimately applied and defended his message in ways that chipped away at the foundation and framework of medieval Catholicism. We can see this simply by looking at his three famous Reformation tracts of 1520—namely, "To the Christian Nobility of the German;" "The Babylonian Captivity of the Church;" and "On Christian Liberty." In these tracts, Luther hammered away at the Roman church in the following ways:

- He redefined the sacramental system. The beliefs and practices of medieval Christians centered upon seven sacraments—namely, baptism, confirmation, penance, the Eucharist, marriage, ordination and extreme unction. Luther ultimately cut the sacraments down to two: baptism and the Eucharist (known by many as the Lord's Supper). Moreover, whereas medieval Catholics insisted that priests repeatedly sacrificed Christ for our sins every time the Lord's Supper was celebrated, Luther argued that Christ's one sacrifice on the cross was unrepeatable and was alone sufficient for the salvation of sinners.

- He challenged the authority of the pope, arguing that both popes and councils could err and that they had erred in the past. He rebutted the claim that only the pope's interpretation of Scripture was authoritative and that only the pope could call together a valid council of the whole church. Moreover, he said that—if the pope refused to bring about a reformation of the church in Germany—the emperor, princes and nobles of the German people had every right, as well as the obligation, to do so since they also were baptized Christians.

- He attacked monasticism and questioned medieval Catholicism's understanding of the priesthood and ministry.

- He argued that canon law—the massive collection of church law that had developed by the 16th century—was not equal with and sometimes even contradicted the law of God as expressed in Scripture.

This is only a short list of the challenges that Luther brought before the Roman church, and a full discussion of each could fill a book. In any case, this should suffice to explain why Luther was condemned in an edict (called a "papal bull") by Pope Leo X in 1520, and why he was summoned—with the promise of a safe conduct—to present himself before the Holy Roman Emperor Charles V at the Diet of Worms in 1521. During this gathering at Worms, Luther stood firm against the majesty of both the Roman church and the Holy Roman Empire.

"Unless I am convicted by Scripture and plain reason, I do not accept the authority of the popes and councils," he said, "for they have contradicted each other. My conscience is captive to the Word of God. I cannot and will not recant anything."[2]

For making this revolutionary stand, Luther was officially condemned as a heretic by Charles V, who nevertheless remained true to his promise of a safe conduct and allowed Luther to return to Wittenberg. Indeed, Luther started the long homeward trek, but his own prince—Frederick 'the Wise' of Saxony—made certain that he was stolen away before his enemies could do him harm. For the next 10 months, he remained in hiding in the Wartburg Castle. But his pen was active even then, and during this relatively short period he translated the New Testament from the original Greek into the High German language.

But when Luther finally came out of hiding in March 1522, he found that his stand against the Roman church had sparked a religious revolution that even he couldn't control.

"
"Preach, pray, but do not fight."

-Martin Luther

8.
AN AFFAIR OF SAUSAGES, A REFORMATION UNTAMED

In early 1522, as Martin Luther lay hidden in central Germany's Wartburg Castle, a Reformation was stirring nearly 330 miles to the southwest in Zurich, a city nestled along the northern fringe of the Swiss Alps. Meanwhile, in Luther's own Wittenberg, matters were moving quickly towards chaos as his university colleagues, in his absence, tried to push forward the religious revolution he had begun.

Luther's call for Reformation had sparked a wildfire that would soon engulf the whole of Western Europe.

An Affair of Sausages

Born high in the Alpine village of Wildhaus, the Swiss Reformer Ulrich Zwingli was inspired by his humanist training to lead the people of Zurich back to the source of their faith: namely,

Scripture. On Jan. 1, 1519, he announced to the congregation of Zurich's Grossmünster that he would break protocol by preaching through Scripture, chapter by chapter, beginning with the Gospel of Matthew. By the time that Luther had gone into hiding at the Wartburg Castle, Zwingli was beginning to pull the people of Zurich away from the Roman church.

The first public, Zwinglian revolt against the Roman church may seem insignificant to us: In March 1522, several of Zwingli's followers gathered together to eat sausages. But, in doing so, they broke the laws of the church, which commanded that Christians should eat only fish during the period of Lent. Although Zwingli abstained from partaking in this "Affair of the Sausages," he entered the pulpit the following Sunday and defended his followers' actions. He delivered a message on Christian freedom, declaring that the church should coerce no one to do something that is not commanded by Scripture.

The "Affair of the Sausages" foreshadowed what was to come in Zurich. During the two years that followed, Zwingli led his followers to cleanse the Zurich church of anything based on human tradition rather than on God's Word. Sculptures were removed from the church and often destroyed; images on the church walls were whitewashed; and, even though Zwingli was a proficient organist, the organ was removed from the Grossmünster. Christian religion in Zurich was purged of anything that was condemned by Scripture or—even more radically—of anything that was not taught by Scripture.

Under Zwingli's guidance, Christians in Zurich thus applied the Reformation principle of sola Scriptura – Scripture alone— to their religious beliefs and practices. But, as will be seen, they applied this principle in a manner that went far beyond what Luther had in mind when he spoke of biblical authority.

Taming the Reformation?

Back in Luther's Wittenberg, the revolt against the Roman church had advanced much in his absence, and it threatened to become uncontrollable. In December 1521, Wittenberg citizens and university students, armed with knives, raided the local parish church, stealing mass books from the altar, thrusting priests from the church and throwing stones at people kneeling in private prayer to the Virgin Mary. From his hideaway, Luther rebuked such violence: "Preach, pray, but do not fight," he wrote.[1]

Nevertheless, riots ensued on Christmas Eve, and the following day Andreas Karlstadt—Luther's elder, and more radical, colleague at the university—preached to a congregation of 2,000 townsfolk (nearly the whole town). He refused to wear traditional clerical garb and, clothed in a simple black robe, broke church tradition by reciting in German Christ's words at the Last Supper and by letting the congregation partake of both the bread and the wine. Under Karlstadt's guidance, all crucifixes, images and statues were removed from the church.

Amid this clamor, more radical preachers came from the nearby town of Zwickau. But they didn't preach a message of sola Scriptura. Instead, they insisted that God had granted them new revelations by the power of the Holy Spirit, apart from Scripture.

When Luther finally was forced out of hiding, he reversed much of Karlstadt's reform efforts. In contrast to both Karlstadt and Zwingli, he restored and promoted the use of religious artwork in churches. In a series of eight sermons, he called upon the reform-minded to restrain themselves and to have patience with those not yet able to endorse the Reformation. He rebuked the "Zwickau prophets" and cast them out of Wittenberg.

Luther desired Reformation, but he also hated disorder. Yet, as seen during Luther's 10 months in hiding, some Reformers insisted upon a more radical view of Christian liberty than he had, as well as a more stringent application of sola Scriptura. Still others dismissed Scripture altogether, preferring their supposedly new, Spirit-inspired, inner revelations.

In short, the Reformation had become untamed.

9.
'THE ARTICLES WHEREFORE JOHN FRITH DIED'

"Amongst all other chances lamentable, there hath been none a great time which seemed unto me more grievous, than the lamentable death and cruel handling of John Frith."

– *John Foxe,* **Book of Martyrs** *(aka,* **Acts and Monuments,** *1570)*[1]

Confined in London's Newgate prison in the summer of 1533, a young English Reformer penned a brief tract with the title, "The Articles Wherefore John Frith Died."[2]

The tract's author, 30-year-old John Frith, had already suffered much for his Reformation beliefs. In 1528, he languished for weeks in an Oxford University fish cellar, where he saw some of his companions die. He then experienced the hardship of exile on the European continent. Later, while on mission in England, he was taken as a vagabond and put in the stocks—fearing for his life, should anyone discover his identity. Only by citing portions of Homer's Iliad in the original Greek from memory did he convince his captors that he was no vagabond, but rather a traveling scholar. So he escaped, this time. On his second mission to England he was imprisoned on charges of heresy. But this time, he was never released.[3]

On July 4, 1533, Frith burned at the stake as a heretic.

But why? Here, we turn to Frith's own account, spelled out in his tract. According to Frith, he would soon die for two reasons: First, he rejected the existence of Purgatory—a fiery netherworld where the souls of baptized Christians would be purged of their sins (See Dante's Divine Comedy for one detailed, literary account of this realm). Frith argued that, through faith in Christ's atoning death on the cross, each Christian's soul is already purged of sin. Moreover, each Christian's flesh is purged of its sinful inclinations through the pains of this life and, ultimately, through death itself. As a result, the Christian has no need for Purgatory after death.

But, ultimately, Frith died for another reason. He died because of Reformation debates surrounding the Lord's Supper—a Christian practice that believers today too often relegate to secondary importance, at best. Frith rejected the belief that Christ's body and blood exist literally within the elements of the Lord's Supper—that is, within the bread and wine. And for this reason, he burned.

To fully grasp what Frith believed and why it matters, we need to consider some background about Reformation debates regarding the Lord's Supper.

Reforming the Lord's Supper

According to the Gospels (as well as the Apostle Paul in 1 Corinthians 11), Christ Jesus taught his disciples to commemorate His death by reenacting together their last dinner with Him. During this dinner, Jesus broke bread and gave it to His disciples, saying, "Take, eat; this is my body." Likewise, He passed a cup to His disciples saying, "Drink of it, all of you, for this is my blood of the covenant, which is poured out for many for the forgiveness of sins" (Matt. 26:26-28, ESV).

During the Middle Ages, a vast body of ceremony and doctrine had developed around the practice of the Lord's Supper. And, during the Reformation, the Lord's Supper became the focus of heated doctrinal debate. By the end of the Reformation, three basic views about this religious ordinance existed:

- Medieval theologians had developed a theory called "*tran*substantiation." According to this theory, the bread and wine used during the Supper were miraculously transformed into the literal, physical body and blood of Jesus. The bread and wine, in fact, no longer existed. Although partakers saw and tasted bread, what they actually ate was the body of Christ. The Roman Catholic Church championed this view during the Reformation period.

- The German Reformer Martin Luther rejected the doctrine of "transubstantiation" as too speculative. Instead, he proposed a new theory that is now called, "*con*substantiation." According to Luther, the bread and the wine used during Communion were just that—bread and wine. Nevertheless, the real, physical body of Christ existed "in, with and under" the bread and wine, somewhat like water is "in, with and under" a sponge.

- In 1525, the Swiss Reformer Ulrich Zwingli entered into public debate with Luther about this issue. Unlike Luther, Zwingli taught that Christ's body and blood were not literally present in the bread and wine used at the Lord's Supper. Instead, he argued that the bread and wine simply symbolized the body and blood of Christ. By partaking of the bread and wine, the faithful meditate on the truth that Jesus' body was broken and His blood was shed once-for-all on the cross. During the Supper, they also looked forward to a day when Christ would bodily return to the earth. Until that day, Jesus is bodily present at the right hand of God the Father.

(On a side note, some of Zwingli's companions and successors would add that, by faith, Christ was spiritually—though not bodily—present in the Lord's Supper. Traditionally, Baptists have affirmed Zwingli's symbolic view of the Supper, although disagreement exists regarding Christ's spiritual presence in the ordinance.)

Luther and Zwingli debated this issue fiercely, and their disagreement would play an important role in carving a deep and lasting divide between the Reformers—that is, between the "Lutheran" and the "Reformed" traditions.

'Nourish, in All Things, Brotherly Love'

Regarding the Lord's Supper, Frith firmly sided with Zwingli and the Reformed tradition. He rejected both Roman Catholic "*tran*substantiation" and Luther's "*con*substantiation."

But he also approached this particular issue with a different spirit than some other Reformers had. In an age of sometimes brutal theological debate, Frith refused to suggest that other Christians were damned heretics for disagreeing with his own view of the Lord's Supper.

"Only avoid idolatry, and we desire no more," Frith once wrote, strongly urging his readers not to sin by worshiping the bread and wine used in the Lord's Supper. Otherwise, he called men and women to search Scripture honestly and believe it firmly— but also charitably. A person on one side of the debate, he said, shouldn't "condemn or despise the other." Rather, everyone should "nourish, in all things, brotherly love," and they should "bear others' infirmities."

Of course, Frith's call for Christian love doesn't mean that he saw doctrinal debates about the Lord's Supper as unimportant. He wouldn't damn or kill another Christian for disagreeing with him in this matter. Nevertheless, for the sake of what he saw as the biblical doctrine of the Lord's Supper, he bravely died.

> "I may err – I am a man – but a heretic I cannot be, because I ask constantly for instruction in the word of God."

-Balthasar Hubmaier

10.

LIVE BY THE SWORD, DIE BY THE SWORD

On July 13, 1524, preaching to various princes in the German city of Allstedt, Thomas Müntzer foretold the end of the ages.

Müntzer interpreted for them the words of the Prophet Daniel as he described the dream of King Nebuchadnezzar (See Daniel 2): In this dream, King Nebuchadnezzar had seen a statue, with a head of gold, chest and arms of silver, stomach and hips of bronze, and feet of mixed iron and clay. As the king looked at the statue, moreover, a stone struck the statue's feet, destroying it completely.

Each section of this statue represented a kingdom, and according to Müntzer the feet of mixed iron and clay represented the godless Christendom of medieval Europe. The stone in Nebuchadnezzar's dream symbolized Christ's godly people, who would take up the sword to overthrow the godless. Müntzer called the princes of Germany to support this cause, warning them that if they refused his call they too "may be slain without mercy."[1]

Referring to himself as "Thomas Müntzer with the Sword of Gideon," this warrior-prophet joined a horde of peasants in May 1525 for what he expected to be the beginning of the end—the overthrow of godless tyrants. In fact, as will be seen below, his own expectations of victory would soon be crushed.

Meanwhile, in the Swiss city of Zurich – where Ulrich Zwingli was pushing ahead his vision of reform – another set of Radical Reformers initiated a peaceful restoration of New Testament Christianity, with an emphasis on the baptism of believers and a life of discipleship.

Thomas Müntzer and the Great Peasants' Revolt

Once a follower of Martin Luther, Müntzer soon became disenchanted with the Wittenberg Reformer. He thought Luther too hesitant in his reform and too dependent on the letter of Scripture. Luther, he said, preached a dead faith, a message empty of spiritual power. He would call Luther by the names of "Brother Hog," "Soft Living Flesh," "Pussyfoot," "Carrion Crow," and "Dr. Liar." And these were more than shallow insults. "With these descriptions he purposed to descry in Luther a sign of the end of the age," wrote historian George Huntston Williams in his classic tome, *The Radical Reformation*.[2]

Anticipating the end of all ages, Müntzer was soon swept up in the "Great Peasants' War" that spread across the Germanic territories of the Holy Roman Empire during the years 1524-1526.

"These uprisings were not a response to Müntzer's incendiary preaching," the late Southern Baptist historian William Estep—himself an expert in the Radical Reformation—wrote in his book, *Renaissance and Reformation*. Instead, he said, "they were the flaming up of long-smoldering discontent that had become increasingly apparent as the nobility, hard-pressed for ready cash, began to take away the traditional privileges and rights of a down-trodden people."[3]

Granted, the peasants of Europe saw a new justification for their cause in Luther's proclamation of Christian liberty, which they understood in social, egalitarian terms. And the more radical, apocalyptic preaching of men like Müntzer only fed the wildfire that was already spreading across Germany.

On May 12, 1525, nearly a year after preaching to the German princes of Allstedt, Müntzer took up the sword for battle, confident that God would vindicate the peasants' cause. Faced by a large army of experienced calvary and foot soldiers, the peasants fought nonetheless.

Prior to their defeat, Müntzer sent a letter to Wittenberg for help. But Luther and his companions ignored his pleas. Indeed, although Luther openly sympathized with some of the peasants' concerns, he also despised rebellion—especially since the rebels distorted his message about Christian liberty. In the spring of 1525, a few weeks after calling German princes to patiently administer justice to the peasants, Luther wrote his tract, "Against the Robbing and Murdering Hordes of Peasants."

"Stab, smite, slay," Luther cried. Anyone who dies fighting against the peasants, he added, dies a martyr's death.[4]

Whether inspired by these words or not, the German princes doubtless ordered their armies to "stab, smite" and "slay." They overthrew the host of peasants whom Müntzer had joined. And, on May 27, 1525, they beheaded Müntzer himself.

The Beginnings of Swiss Anabaptism

Earlier, soon after hearing about Müntzer's sermon before the German princes in Allstedt, a group of radical Swiss reformers—led especially by a man named Conrad Grebel—sent Müntzer a letter.

This was their second letter to the revolutionary prophet. In an earlier letter, sent during the fall of 1524, they insisted that people shouldn't "protect the gospel and its adherents with the sword." But at that time, they believed that Müntzer taught likewise. As soon as they heard about Müntzer's revolutionary preaching, they wrote to him again, urging him to "desist" immediately.[5]

Grebel and some of his companions would soon become leaders among the first Swiss Anabaptists—a group of Radical Reformers who broke away from Reformer Ulrich Zwingli of Zurich, Switzerland, by denying the validity of infant baptism. And like their modern-day descendants among the Mennonites, these early Anabaptists would come to champion pacifism. Yet, according to historian Harold Bender, their "Anabaptist Vision" was ultimately rooted in discipleship:

"The true test of the Christian, they held, is discipleship," he wrote. "The great word of the Anabaptists was not 'faith' as it was with the reformers, but 'following' (Nachfolge Christi). And baptism, the greatest of the Christian symbols, was accordingly to be for them the 'covenant of a good conscience toward God' (1 Peter 3:21), the pledge of a complete commitment to obey Christ, and not primarily the symbol of a past experience."[6]

On Jan. 21, 1525, while meeting in the home of Felix Manz, Grebel put into practice this vision when he baptized George Blaurock upon his profession of faith. In turn, Blaurock baptized Grebel, Manz and others who so desired. With these first believers' baptisms of the Reformation period, Swiss Anabaptism was born.

Yet, because they submitted to believers' baptism and to a life of discipleship, these early Anabaptists soon experienced what Grebel had previously written to Müntzer: "True believing Christians are sheep among wolves, sheep for the slaughter. They must be baptized in anxiety, distress, affliction, persecution, suffering, and death."[7] Indeed, by 1529, these leaders of the early Anabaptist movement would be dead, having endured severe persecution for their beliefs even at the hands of Protestant Reformers. Whereas the revolutionary Müntzer both lived and died by the sword, they took up their crosses and followed Christ Jesus to the very end.

> *"Where there is no water baptism, there is no church nor minister, neither brother nor sister, no brotherly admonition, excommunication, or reacceptance."*

–Balthasar Hubmaier

11.
'TRUTH IS IMMORTAL'

Once called the "Simon Peter" of the early Anabaptist movement, Balthasar Hubmaier fled from the city of Zurich in secrecy and shame in 1526.[1]

In that city, where Reformer Ulrich Zwingli's teachings held sway, Hubmaier faced imprisonment and torture before finally denying his belief that only those who have professed faith in Christ and surrendered to a life of discipleship should be baptized. For this reason, the leaders of Zurich released Hubmaier, disgraced before both his enemies and his friends. After fleeing the city, he wrote the following words in a confession that he called, "A Short Apology":

"I may err – I am a man – but a heretic I cannot be, because I ask constantly for instruction in the word of God. But never has any one come to me and pointed out a single word, but one single man [that is, Zwingli] and his followers … by capture, imprisonment, sufferings and the hangman, tried to teach me the faith. But faith is a work of God and not of the heretic's tower, in which one sees neither sun nor moon, and lives on nothing but water and bread. … O God, pardon me my weakness. It is good for me (as David says) that thou hast humbled me."[2]

In this confession, Hubmaier revealed his humble reliance on God's word. Admitting his own weakness and faithlessness, he knew that God would always remain faithful and that His truth would stand forever.

Transformed by Truth

Born in the town of Friedburg, Germany, in the 1480s, Hubmaier showed promise within the late medieval Catholic church. In fact, he earned a doctorate in theology under John Eck—who was one of Martin Luther's most formidable opponents during the early Reformation.

Hubmaier also showed promise as a medieval priest, according to the late Southern Baptist historian William Estep in his classic book, *The Anabaptist Story*. "During thunderstorms he stationed himself at the church door with the Host [that is, the bread consecrated for use in the Lord's Supper] and blessed the clouds," Estep writes. "At Easter and on other occasions, as when the Host was carried to the sick, he saw that everything was done with much pomp and ceremony."[3]

While serving as the people's priest in the city of Regensburg, Hubmaier also championed a tragic – yet typically medieval – campaign against Jews. Inspired partially by his preaching, the city pushed out its Jewish population and transformed the former synagogue into a Catholic chapel dedicated "to the beauteous Mary."[4] The chapel would become a hugely popular pilgrimage site.

Although Hubmaier could have had a successful career within the Catholic church, he would ultimately follow a different path. In the early 1520s, Hubmaier started reading Scripture, especially the letters of Paul. He began to accept Reformation ideas—first, those of Martin Luther, although he would ultimately be more sympathetic with the ideas of Ulrich

Zwingli in Zurich. Soon, he implemented reform in the city of Waldshut, where he then served as a priest, and he took the Reformation further than either Luther or Zwingli would be willing to do. He began to baptize only believers.

As one of the few Anabaptists to have a doctorate in theology, Hubmaier became a natural leader within the movement. His writings in support of believer's baptism would be read by Anabaptists for decades. His most famous defense of this practice, "On the Christian Baptism of Believers," would still be in circulation a century later.

Hubmaier insisted that only faith can justify, and the outward practice of baptism has no spiritual power to save us. However, he saw baptism as an essential part of the Christian life.

"Where there is no water baptism, there is no church nor minister, neither brother nor sister, no brotherly admonition, excommunication, or reacceptance," Hubmaier wrote. "I am speaking here of the visible church as Christ did in Matthew 18:15ff. There must also exist an outward confession or testimony through which visible brothers and sisters can know each other, since faith exists only in the heart. But when he receives the baptism of water the one who is baptized testifies publicly that he has pledged himself henceforth to live according to the Rule of Christ."[5]

Hubmaier also proclaimed that no one should be forced into faith at the point of the sword, since only the gospel can produce faith. Instead of persecuting Jews, Pagans and heretics, Christians should love them and try to correct them through the preaching and teaching of God's word. In his work, "On Heretics and Those Who Burn Them," he writes, "Now it is apparent to everyone, even the blind, that the law which demands the burning of heretics is an invention of the Devil." Following this statement, Hubmaier penned a declaration that would characterize both his writings and his life: "Truth is Immortal."[6]

Mortal Man, Immortal Truth

Because of his stance on believer's baptism, Hubmaier would come into conflict with Zwingli, who tried to refute Hubmaier's teaching with his pen and also—as noted above—through torture. Although the Anabaptist leader was forced out of Zurich in shame in 1526, he repented of his faithlessness amid persecution, and he began again to proclaim the truth in the Moravian city of Nikolsburg. With support from local rulers, he may have baptized as many as 6,000 believers in his one brief year of ministry in the city.

Yet Hubmaier was soon arrested once more—this time by the Catholic authorities in Austria. And this time he would remain faithful to the truth of Scripture even amid persecution. On March 10, 1528, he was burned at the stake. Three days later, his faithful wife—Elizabeth—was drowned in the Danube river.

By faithfulness in his death, Hubmaier lived out the truth of baptism, as he described it in his final appeal to the authorities in Austria: "I have taught nothing else regarding baptism except that it is a public and oral confession of the Christian faith, and a renunciation that one must address to the devil and his works, so that a person, in the power of God the Father and the Son and the Holy Spirit, may yield himself in such surrender that he is willing with Christ to suffer, die, and be buried, in the faith that he will arise with him to everlasting life."[7]

In this faith, Hubmaier died, confident that the immortal truth of God's word would stand forever.

12

DID BAPTISTS GROW FROM ANABAPTIST SEED?

At one Anabaptist museum in Austria, visitors can see the chains with which Anabaptist women were shackled to their homes. Without their husbands' consent, these women had accepted the Anabaptist message and were baptized. Yet, in these instances, the women were allowed to live, since their husbands needed them to raise their children and tend to their homes. But they would do so in chains.

These chains remind us of the intense persecution that the 16th-century Anabaptists suffered. Indeed, many women suffered for this cause; roughly one-third of the 900 Anabaptists mentioned in the Martyrs Mirror—a sort of Anabaptist book of martyrs, written in the 1600s—were women. Yet these women didn't suffer alone.

Catholics and Protestants alike were intent on wiping out Anabaptism. They persecuted anyone who accepted or, especially, preached the Anabaptist message, seeing this so-called heresy as a spiritual disease that threatened the souls of men and women, as well as the stability of society. As such, Anabaptists were tortured, mocked, starved, imprisoned, beheaded, burned and drowned. And many Anabaptists expected nothing less than to suffer for their faith.

"It is surely true that as soon as one wants to begin living as a Christian, one experiences none other than Christ experienced," Anabaptist Leonhard Schiemer once wrote. "It is to this that you are called, for Christ also suffered and left us an example, to follow in his footsteps."

In 1527, Schiemer himself was imprisoned for seven weeks during a bitter Alpine winter before being beheaded and then burned. Partly because of Schiemer's courage amid suffering, Pilgram Marpeck—who would become one of the few Anabaptist leaders to die naturally—soon accepted believer's baptism. Marpeck later wrote that every follower of Christ must submit "to the fellowship of suffering under God's hand and discipline."

Schiemer, Marpeck and other Anabaptists had confidence that—in the words of Tertullian, a theologian of the early church—"the blood of the martyrs is the seed of the church." But in the case of the Anabaptists, one may ask, "Which church?" Did any modern-day churches grow from the seed planted by the persecuted Anabaptists? Do modern-day Baptists themselves have Anabaptist roots?

Did the Anabaptist Seed Grow into the Baptist Church?

Doubtless, the answer to the first question is, "Yes." Several religious groups throughout the world can claim an Anabaptist ancestry. Among them are the Mennonites (named after the 16th-century Anabaptist, Menno Simons); the Hutterites (named after 16th-century Anabaptist Jacob Hutter); and the Amish (named after 17th-century Anabaptist Jacob Amman).[1]

Yet the second question mentioned above is more complicated. In fact, historians have long debated whether the Baptist movement—which grew up in England nearly 100 years after the Reformation began—was influenced in any way by the Anabaptists.

This historical debate can be quite complex and nitty-gritty, looking even at indirect influences that the Anabaptists may have had on the later Baptists: For example, one historian has suggested that the Reformed emphasis on church discipline, which was later adopted by the English Baptists, was originally developed in response to the Anabaptist emphasis on church discipline.[2]

Amid this complexity, one can safely say that the Anabaptists drew a line in the sand regarding some important truths of Scripture, and Baptists—whether they realized it or not—later sided with the Anabaptists regarding these truths.

"The Anabaptists of the Reformation have much to teach contemporary Baptists," Paige Patterson, president of Southwestern Baptist Theological Seminary, said in 2012 during a conference on "Anabaptism and Contemporary Baptists."[3] He went on to note that, however interesting it may be, the question about the historical connection between Baptists and Anabaptists is really of little consequence. Nevertheless, he added, the Anabaptists championed five convictions that Baptists today should defend:

- First, the Anabaptists dedicated themselves to the Reformation truth of sola Scriptura. While they shared this conviction about the supremacy of Scripture with other Reformers, the Anabaptists uniquely believed that the church should be shaped after the New Testament model—a truth that impacted their support of believer's baptism and their beliefs about the relationship between the church and civil authorities.

- Second, the Anabaptists emphasized the believer's church, which consists only of people who are baptized after professing faith in Jesus. In baptism, they publicly yielded themselves to a life of discipleship, making themselves accountable not only to God, but also to the encouragement and discipline of the congregation.
- Third, the Anabaptists submitted themselves and their congregations to Christ Jesus, who alone is Lord.
- Fourth, the Anabaptists endorsed religious liberty and insisted that the civil authorities shouldn't tamper with the church or its theology.

"The Anabaptists were the first ones to question the whole concept that to be a citizen was to be a churchman and to be a churchman was to be a citizen," Southern Baptist church historian James Leo Garrett once said. "The Christian society of Europe was one, and church and state were one. The religion of the ruler would be the religion of the people. In most places, that was the case. The Anabaptists challenged that whole idea."

- Finally, the Anabaptists exemplified how Christians should stay true to the faith even amid persecution.

"Completely surrender to God under his cross," one Anabaptist wrote. "Accept the suffering, persecution, and cross, inward and outward, which will result and will not fail to come to you. Such is the school of Christ into which he calls all who want to become his disciples."

(Much of the content in this chapter has been adapted from articles that I wrote for the Fall 2012 edition of Southwestern News, the alumni magazine of Southwestern Baptist Theological Seminary in Fort Worth, Texas. I learned about the suffering of Anabaptist women from an article written in the same magazine by my former colleague, Sharayah Colter, who now serves as a writer with the Southern Baptist TEXAN).

13.

A MINISTRY OF WORD AND SPIRIT

By the spring of 1539, John Calvin had been twice-exiled.

First, he had been forced to leave his beloved homeland, France. At one time, having fostered Christian humanism within its borders, this kingdom seemed ripe for receiving the Reformation ideas of men like Martin Luther in Germany or Ulrich Zwingli in Zurich. But in the early 1530s, the tide began to turn against reform-minded Frenchmen like Calvin, and in the decades to come the Protestant Reformation would be violently suppressed within France.

Second, shortly after the Easter of 1538, Calvin and his colleagues were cast out of Geneva, a border city, nestled between France to the west and the Swiss Confederacy to the east. Calvin had never intended to involve himself in efforts to reform Geneva. But while taking a detour through the city in 1536, the outspoken French preacher William Farel tried to persuade Calvin to stay in the city and use his abilities for the sake of Christ's cause.

Calvin later recalled this encounter with Farel: "When he realized that I was determined to study in privacy in some obscure place and saw that he gained nothing by entreaty, he descended to cursing, and said that God would surely curse my peace if I held back from giving help at a time of such great need."[1]

"Terrified by his words, and conscious of my own timidity and cowardice," Calvin added, "I gave up my journey and attempted to apply whatever gift I had in defense of my faith."[2]

So he joined Farel as a preacher in the city. But in 1538, caught in a muddle of theological and political debates, both preachers were ousted from Geneva. Calvin then traveled to the Swiss city of Strasbourg, where he served as a pastor to French refugees.

But in March 1539, the Catholic church beckoned Genevan officials to restore the city's allegiance to Rome, thinking that they could be convinced to do so in the absence of Farel and Calvin's leadership. This call came in the form of a letter from Cardinal Jacopo Sadoleto, an upstanding and scholarly archbishop within the Roman church.

Desperate to find a theologian who could answer Sadoleto's letter, Genevan officials turned to their former preacher. Calvin's "Reply to Sadoleto" is a classic outline of Reformation teaching, a must-read even for Christians who can't agree with every aspect of his theology.

In his letter, Sadoleto urged the Genevans to return to the papal church, arguing that this church was the true church that had always been "directed by the one Spirit of Christ."[3] But in reply, Calvin accused Sadoleto of wrongly severing God's Spirit from God's Word. After all, how could the Roman church claim to be guided by the Spirit, when it rejected the truths of Scripture, such as the doctrine of justification by faith alone?

Christ's true church is, indeed, guided by the Holy Spirit, Calvin said. But, to establish the church with the stability and clarity of truth, the Lord "annexed" the Holy Spirit to the Word of God. The Word of God, he said, is the litmus that "tests all doctrines," and the Spirit of God guides the church only by the means of His Word.[4]

After Calvin faithfully defended the Reformation in this reply, the Genevans pled with him to return to the city as their pastor. In the fall of 1541, therefore, he returned to Geneva, devoting the remainder of his life to establishing godly worship and piety within the city. Convinced that this could be done only by the power of the Spirit working through the Word, he also devoted himself to expounding Scripture.

In fact, between 1541 and 1564, he preached through the books of "Psalms, Jeremiah, Lamentations, Micah, Zephaniah, Joel, Amos, Obadiah, Jonah, Daniel, Ezekiel, 1 and 2 Thessalonians, 1 and 2 Timothy, Titus, 1 and 2 Corinthians, Job, Deuteronomy, Isaiah, Galatians, Ephesians, Harmony of the Gospels, Acts, Genesis, Judges, 1 and 2 Samuel, and 1 Kings." He preached 200 sermons on the book of Deuteronomy alone, as well as 174 on Ezekiel and 189 on Acts.

Throughout his ministry, beginning even before he returned to Geneva, Calvin also wrote commentaries on the New Testament and on much of the Old Testament. Of course, in doing so, he joined the company of other reform-minded biblical scholars, such as Martin Bucer of Strasbourg. But Bucer's biblical exegesis was interlaced with so many in-depth and lengthy theological summaries that his commentaries became unwieldy.

In contrast, Calvin's commentaries were brief and focused primarily on discovering what the biblical author intended to say to the reader. He was able to achieve such brevity and focus in his commentaries because of another work that he labored on throughout his life—namely, his well-known Institutes of the Christian Religion. First published in 1536, the Institutes were republished several times and greatly expanded by 1560. One modern-day English translation of the work contains more than 1500 pages in 2 volumes.

Calvin's Institutes provides a comprehensive introduction to Christian theology. He hoped it would "be a key to open a way for all children of God into a good and right understanding of Holy Scripture." This work, he added, would allow him to write commentaries with "the greatest possible brevity, because there will be no need for long digressions, seeing that I have here treated at length almost all the articles pertaining to Christianity."[6]

So even in this massive theological tome, the Genevan Reformer had his eye on the centrality and supremacy of Scripture. God's Word, he wrote in the Institutes, was "a special gift" given by God to "instruct the church." In Scripture, God "opens his own most hallowed lips" to teach us and—through the power of His Spirit, working by the Word—to transform us.[7]

14

CALVIN AND THE CALVINISTS

When Martin Luther pinned (or pasted) his 95 Theses on the church door in Wittenberg in 1517, John Calvin was only 8 years old.

By the time Calvin published the first edition of his classic *Institutes of the Christian Religion* in 1536, Ulrich Zwingli—the Reformer of Zurich—had been dead for five years, having been cut down in battle against the city's Catholic opponents in 1531.

Multiple pathways for reform had been carved out across the European landscape before Calvin even entered the Reformation fray. Nevertheless, this second-generation Reformer stamped his name upon one of the main branches of Reformation thought—namely, the Reformed tradition, known also as "Calvinism." According to some Reformation scholars today, however, "Calvinism" is a misnomer for several reasons:

First, Calvin was by no means the founder of "Calvinism." In fact, no one person founded the Reformed tradition in the manner that Luther founded the Lutheran tradition.[1]

Nevertheless, several theologians and leaders made a significant impact on the Reformed tradition even before Calvin came out in public support of Reformation ideas. These leaders of an earlier generation include not only Zwingli, but also:

- **Martin Bucer**, a Reformer in the city of Strassburg, who had been drawn to Luther's ideas as early as 1518 and who ended his days as an exile in England, teaching a new generation of Protestant leaders at Cambridge University: his impact was extensive, and Calvin himself served for a brief time as a pastor to French Refugees in Strassburg, where he was able in a manner to sit at Bucer's feet;

- **John Oecolampadius**, a friend of the well-known humanist Erasmus and a leader of the Reformation in the city of Basel, who died in 1531 only a few weeks after Zwingli did;

- and **William Farel**, the fiery preacher from France who threatened Calvin with a divine curse should he opt for a peaceful life of scholarship instead of using his gifts to help bring Reform to the city of Geneva (needless to say, Calvin opted to avoid the divine curse).

Second, as Reformation historian Richard Muller points out, "the vast majority of 16th- and 17th-century thinkers we identify as Calvinists did not identify themselves as followers of Calvin."[2] These include Calvin's influential contemporaries like Heinrich Bullinger (Zwingli's successor in Zurich) or the Italian Reformer Peter Martyr Vermigli; and later theologians, including Calvin's own successor in Geneva, Theodore Beza.

Third, some theologians and historians have debated whether Calvin himself could be considered a "Calvinist"—especially if you define the term "Calvinism" by belief in the popular (or, depending on one's theological views, infamous) T-U-L-I-P acronym. For example, some scholars doubt that Calvin would have affirmed the 21st-century "Calvinist" doctrine of "limited atonement" (the "L" in the T-U-L-I-P acronym). This debate rages on today, and I'm neither able nor willing to settle it in this column. Regardless, the debate exemplifies the problems and questions that arise when considering the relationship between Calvin and "Calvinism."[3]

Fourth, as Reformation historian Carl Trueman has noted, the Reformed tradition isn't enshrined in the works of any one theologian; rather, it is expressed in various confessional documents. Each of these confessional documents were formulated for different reasons and in the context of specific political situations and theological controversies. They include the Second Helvetic, Gallican, Belgic and Scots confessions, the 39 Articles of the Church of England, the Canons of Dort and the Westminster Confession of Faith.[4]

It may be worthwhile to end this column by quoting another of these confessional documents—namely, the Heidelberg Catechism of 1563. This catechism was, of course, written in a Q&A format to aide in one-on-one teaching. It begins with a beautiful statement of gospel truth that has been handed down through the ages—a statement that even many non-Calvinists could appreciate:

> "Q: What is thy only comfort in life and death?
>
> "A: That I with body and soul, both in life and death, am not my own, but belong unto my faithful Saviour Jesus Christ; who, with his precious blood, has fully satisfied for all my sins, and delivered me from all the power of the devil; and so preserves me that without the will of my heavenly Father, not a hair can fall from my head; yea, that all things must be subservient to

my salvation; and therefore, by his Holy Spirit, He also assures me of eternal life, and makes me sincerely willing and ready, henceforth, to live unto him."[5]

Doubtless, whether or not this document should be called "Calvinist," Calvin himself would have agreed with this statement wholeheartedly.

15.
CATHOLIC RENEWAL AND REACTION

In our fascination with the theological debates of the Reformation period, we often forget how much turned during this era on the mundane, political events that had very little direct connection with theological or spiritual matters.

Take, for example, the Battle of Pamplona of May 20, 1521. The battle itself had nothing to do with religion or theology. It was merely one battle among many in a series of wars sparked by attempts of the Holy Roman Emperor Charles V and the French King Francis I to gain the upper hand over one another in European politics. Nevertheless, this battle would have a profound impact for shaping the Roman Catholic Church's own attempts to find religious renewal and its ability to counteract the Protestant Reformation.

During a siege of the city of Pamplona, a canon ball struck a Basque nobleman named Iñigo Lopez de Loyola (better known as Ignatius Loyola), shattering not only his leg but also the worldly ambitions he had been pursuing as a soldier. Forced into a long recuperation, Loyola began to read traditional works of Catholic devotion, such as the *Life of Christ*, the *Golden Legend*, and later Thomas a Kempis' *Imitation of Christ*. Through his encounter with these works, Loyola eventually had a sort of conversion—dedicating himself now as a soldier in the service of Christ Jesus and his Mother.

Eventually, although he had not become a monk, Loyola embarked on an ascetic lifestyle and went on pilgrimage to Jerusalem. After returning to Europe, however, he was confronted by the Inquisition for holding suspicious beliefs.

Infamous for its supposedly brutal suppression of heresy, the Inquisition first developed in Spain as a way to prosecute those suspected of Jewish or Muslim beliefs, as well as pre-Reformation heresies. It was, according to Reformation historian Carter Lindberg, a "tool of social control against outsiders." The brutality of the Inquisition has often been exaggerated in the modern imagination – although not without reason, since it would sometimes use torture against its captives. However, according to Lindberg, the Inquisition primarily used the fear of public shame to squelch heresy. In any case, the Inquisition became a defensive bulwark against the Protestant Reformation, and it explains—though only in part—why the Reformation never made any significant inroads into Spain.[1]

The Reformation failed in Spain also because there had been a movement of renewal within the Spanish church, led by Archbishop Francisco Jimenez de Cisneros, who died in 1517— the same year that Martin Luther posted his *95 Theses* and ignited the Reformation. Because of this renewal movement, the Spanish church was less exposed than other European churches to the attacks of Reformers, who protested the immorality and ignorance of the clergy. Jimenez made efforts to remove such abuses, and he was able to combine—though only temporarily—traditional Spanish Catholicism with the Christian humanist (not to be confused with modern-day secular humanist) appeal to textual scholarship and personal devotion. In fact, he founded three universities and sponsored the Complutensian Polyglot—a massive work of scholarship that placed the Latin Vulgate translation of Scripture side-by-side with the original Hebrew and Greek texts, as well as the ancient Greek translation and Aramaic paraphrase of the Old Testament.[2]

Given this context of spiritual renewal, it is no wonder that Spain would produce a man—namely, Loyola—who would play a large role in renewing and defending the traditional Catholic faith.

Having convinced the Inquisition of his orthodoxy, Loyola went on to establish a new religious order, the Society of Jesus (also called the Jesuits). He and his original band of followers initially wanted to take a pilgrimage to the Holy Lands to defend the faith there. But, after their journey was waylaid by political events, they instead went to Rome and offered their services to the pope.

Although Loyola didn't establish the Society of Jesus to rebuff the Protestant Reformation, the Roman church would soon find that the Jesuits were indispensable in their efforts to win back the territories that had been lost to Protestantism. This was the case for three reasons: First, unlike other religious orders, the Jesuits were not bound to one location. Instead, they were active and mobile, enabling them to spread their message not only across Europe, but also around the world. According to Lindberg, by 1626 there were 15,000 Jesuits spread across the globe—in areas such as India, Africa, Brazil, Japan and China—by 1626.[3] The missionary endeavors of the Jesuits were featured on the big screen in 2016 in the Martin Scorsese film, *Silence*.

Second, the Jesuits developed an effective educational system, thus giving the Roman church a way of keeping young people in the Catholic faith.

Finally, the Society of Jesus was devoted staunchly to serving the Roman Catholic Church. This is indicated by a classic Catholic devotional work written by Loyola, the *Spiritual Exercises*. This work primarily mapped out Loyola's program for spiritual transformation through meditation and submission to God. However, he made it clear that submission to God entailed submission to the Roman church. He wrote,

"If we wish to proceed securely in all things, we must hold fast to the following principle: What seems to me white, I will believe black if the hierarchical Church so defines. For I must be convinced that in Christ our Lord, the bridegroom, and in His spouse the Church, only one Spirit holds sway, which governs and rules for the salvation of souls. For it is by the same Spirit and Lord who gave the Ten Commandments that our holy Mother Church is ruled and governed."[4]

Because of this conviction, the Jesuits would become an invaluable tool as the Roman church established its Counter-Reformation, which will be discussed further in the next chapter.

16.

ROMAN CATHOLIC COUNTER-REFORMATION

As early as 1519, Martin Luther called for the gathering of a general council to reform the church, rebuffing the Roman church's claim that only the pope could convene a valid council.

A decade later, no council had been called. And in 1529 Thomas More, defending the Roman church, complained that Luther appealed to a general council merely "to seek a long delay." More's opponent, the English Reformer William Tyndale, soon offered a reply: "Of a truth that were a long delay. For should Martin (Luther) live till the pope gathered a council in the Holy Ghost, or for any godly purpose, he were like to be for every hair of his head a thousand years old."[1]

By no means a trivial matter, Luther's demand for a general council would have reminded his readers how, in the previous two centuries, such councils challenged the authority of the pope and attempted—though in vain—to reform the church. But ultimately the Fifth Lateran Council, meeting on the eve of the Reformation (1512-1517), did little to reform the church and actually reaffirmed the pope's authority.[2] As such, the pope was not about to relinquish his authority by letting anyone convene a council against his will.

So, even though Luther wouldn't have to wait millennia to see a council convened, he would have to wait decades. Meanwhile, some Reformers and Catholics alike tried to bring healing and restore unity to the church. During the Imperial Diet of Regensburg, which opened in 1541, leaders from both sides of the debate gathered to find a middle way. At first, there was some hope that they would be able to come to an agreement even on the key issue of justification by faith alone, but ultimately both sides rejected compromise and the split between Reformers and Catholics only widened.

The following year, Pope Paul III finally called for the gathering of a general council—though, had he been alive, Tyndale would doubtless have questioned this pope's intent or ability to gather a council "in the Holy Ghost, or for any godly purpose." In 1545, the year before Luther's death, the council convened in the city of Trent. Meeting intermittently over a 20-year span, the Council of Trent hardened the Roman church's opposition to the Protestant Reformers.

The Council of Trent did attempt to reform the Roman church by clarifying its teachings and by responding to various abuses—such as immorality and lack of education among clergymen—that Protestants had often criticized. However, when addressing theological matters that were central to the debates of the Reformation period, the council unquestionably opposed the Protestant Reformers:

- First, the council questioned the Protestant principle of *sola Scriptura* (that is, the supreme authority of Scripture). Members of the council declared that the truth of God is "contained in the *written books* and in the *unwritten traditions*," each of which were received from the apostles, inspired and preserved by the Holy Spirit, and passed down from age to age in the institutional church.[3]

As for Scripture itself, the council insisted that the Latin Vulgate is "authentic" and authoritative, and that "no one dare or presume under any pretext whatsoever to reject it." Moreover, they said, no one should "presume to interpret" Scripture "contrary to that sense which holy mother Church … has held and holds, or even contrary to the unanimous teaching of the Fathers."[4]

- Second, the council rejected the Protestant principle of *sola fide* (that is, justification by faith alone, apart from good works). "If anyone says that the sinner is justified by faith alone," they declared, "let him be anathema."[5]

- Third, the council reaffirmed the medieval doctrine of the Lord's Supper, called transubstantiation. They ruled that, when the bread and wine are consecrated by a priest, the substance of the bread is transformed "into the substance of the body of Christ our Lord" and the wine "into the substance of His blood."[6]

The council damned each of the Reformation views of the Lord's Supper: namely, the Zwinglian and Anabaptist view that the bread and wine are only symbols of Christ's body and blood; Luther's view that Christ's body and blood are substantially and really present alongside, around and within the bread and the wine; and the view, expressed by Calvin and some other Reformed thinkers, that Christ's presence in the Lord's Supper was only spiritual.

The canons and decrees of the Council of Trent established Roman Catholicism upon the foundation of the medieval theological system of Thomas Aquinas, and it shaped Catholicism for centuries to come. Yet Tridentine Catholicism—as Catholicism following the Council of

Trent is often called—wasn't a mere replica of the medieval Catholic church. Instead, it was a Catholicism defined in opposition to the Protestant Reformation. It was a church of the Counter-Reformation.[7]

17.
STRANGE BEDFELLOWS OF THE ENGLISH REFORMATION

The story of the English Reformation begins with the stuff of legend. For, in 1485, the Welshman Henry Tudor landed with his armies on the English coast, defeated King Richard III in battle at Bosworth Field, and was proclaimed King Henry VII. Through his marriage with the daughter of an earlier king, he guaranteed his security on the throne and claimed to reunite England after decades of dynastic conflict. Then, in 1486, the new king welcomed his first son into the world, naming him after the mythical Arthur of Camelot—thus establishing his right to rule England on popular legend.[1]

But this legendary tale wouldn't last. The young prince Arthur was promised at an early age in marriage to the Spanish princess Catherine of Aragon. The young couple celebrated their marriage ceremony in 1501—but too late for prince Arthur, who was declining in health and died the following year.

Arthur's younger brother, Henry, was now heir to the throne of England. Church law wouldn't normally allow a man to marry his brother's widow, but Pope Julius II granted a dispensation allowing prince Henry to marry Catherine of Aragon in order to maintain the political alliance between Spain and England. The couple were married in 1509, only about nine weeks after prince Henry ascended to the throne of England following his father's death. In time, this marriage would drive the English church from its allegiance to the Roman papacy.

After coming to the throne, the flamboyant King Henry VIII tried to gain chivalric honor and power within European politics. Holding to traditional Catholic beliefs, he didn't hesitate to attack the German Reformer Martin Luther in a 1521 tract that earned him an honorary title from the pope: "Defender of the Faith."[2]

William Tyndale, Thomas More and the English Bible

Meanwhile, in southwest England, William Tyndale—an Oxford graduate and priest—came into conflict with a "learned man" who claimed it would be better to live without God's law than without the pope's laws. At this, Tyndale cried out, "I defy the pope and all his laws. If God spare my life, ere many years I will cause a boy that driveth the plough to know more of the Scripture than thou dost."[3]

This declaration would define both Tyndale's life and death. After vainly seeking a sponsor for his Bible translation in the church, Tyndale left England, going first to Luther's own Wittenberg and then to the city of Cologne, where he began to print an English translation of the New Testament. But, after being discovered by the authorities, he fled to Worms, where he finally published in 1526 the first complete English New Testament to be translated from the original Greek.

Tyndale later published the first five books of the Old Testament (also called the Pentateuch), translated from Hebrew, but was unable to complete his Old Testament translation before being betrayed to his death.

In 1529, the year before Tyndale printed the Pentateuch, Thomas More—an English lawyer who was on the king's council and who would soon be named Lord Chancellor of England—wrote a lengthy dialogue attacking evangelical heretics like Luther and Tyndale. Soon Tyndale responded with a brief answer to More's dialogue. And, again, More replied with a *Confutation of Tyndale's Answer*, a work that trudged along for half a million venomous words.

Ironically, Tyndale may have considered More, the famous author of *The Utopia*, a friend of reform little more than a decade earlier. Indeed, he felt betrayed by More's attacks. But, although he was friendly with famous Christian humanists and was no particular lover of the pope, More always believed that the hierarchical Roman church was the only guarantor of truth and order in the world. If the church falls, the world will collapse into chaos. Thus, the church must be defended vehemently.

It is no wonder then that some—though not all—historians have argued that More himself employed Henry Phillips, who betrayed Tyndale to his death. In October 1536, after being imprisoned and tried by Catholic authorities in the Belgian city of Vilvoorde, Tyndale—a martyr for Reformation truths—was strangled and then burned at the stake.

But by the time of Tyndale's death, More had been dead for a year—a Catholic martyr beheaded by the authority of King Henry VIII.[4]

But why did More die?

Strange Bedfellows: The King's 'Great Matter' and More's Death

Church historian E. Gordon Rupp once observed that the English Reformation brought together some strange "bedfellows," and none stranger than Tyndale and More—enemies who both opposed King Henry VIII in his "great matter."[5]

In the late 1520s and early 1530s, King Henry VIII became concerned since his wife, Catherine of Aragon, hadn't yet given him a son to rule England after his death. His conscience was struck by the words of Leviticus 20:21, which reads in the King James Version, "And if a man shall take his brother's wife, it *is* an unclean thing: he hath uncovered his brother's nakedness; they shall be childless." Had he therefore sinned against God by marrying his brother's widow?

Answering Henry's question in 1530, Tyndale explained that the king hadn't sinned and that Leviticus 20:21 only prohibited adultery with a living brother's wife. The king's marriage with Queen Catherine was valid and biblical.

But the king wasn't satisfied by such an answer—especially since he'd already set his eyes on his next queen, a young woman in court named Anne Boleyn. But, though Tyndale refused to support his annulment, Henry VIII ironically had the support of other reform-minded Englishmen. So, when he saw that the pope wouldn't release him from his marriage with Catherine, he cut off the English church's allegiance to the pope, had his marriage with Catherine annulled, and led Parliament to declare that the king was the "Supreme Head" of the church in England.

Like Tyndale, yet for different reasons, More had misgivings about the "great matter" of the king's annulment. And when Henry VIII made such drastic moves against the church, More stepped down from his post as Lord Chancellor and tried to protect himself with silence. But after Parliament required oaths from English citizens in favor of the king's marriage and headship over the church, More was arrested for refusing the oath. In the end, he was condemned as a traitor and beheaded.

Thus, by 1536, both Tyndale and More were dead—foes in life, but bedfellows in their opposition to the king's "great matter."

"

"The Scriptures spring out of God and flow unto Christ, and were given to lead us to Christ. Thou must therefore go along by the Scripture as by a line, until thou come at Christ, which is the way's end and resting place."

-William Tyndale

18.
'THAT WE FINALLY LOSE NOT THE THINGS ETERNAL'

"God (the protector of all that trust in thee, without whom nothing is strong, nothing is holy), increase and multiply upon us thy mercy, that thou being our ruler and guide, we may so pass through things temporal that we finally lose not the things eternal; grant this, heavenly Father, for Jesus Christ's sake our Lord. Amen."

– The English Book of Common Prayer, 1549[1]

On the night of March 17, 1556, Thomas Cranmer, once Archbishop of Canterbury and now a prisoner condemned to die, slept. And as he slept, he dreamed. And in his dream, there stood before him two kings: his late master, King Henry VIII, and the eternal King Jesus Christ. As an early account of this dream tells us, Cranmer "had sought the goodwill of one of them in a life which was often chasing after power; from the other he pleaded for help after death."[2]

Indeed, throughout his life, Cranmer had sought the goodwill of King Henry VIII, and he received it. In the late 1520s and early 1530s—as Henry VIII sought to dissolve his marriage with his first wife, Catherine of Aragon—the young Cranmer pleased Henry by proposing that the king turn to the universities of Europe for support. Then, while Cranmer was on the European continent promoting the king's cause, he was ordained Archbishop of Canterbury and was recalled to England, where he soon officiated the public wedding of Henry VIII and his new queen, Anne Boleyn.

Cranmer sympathized with the Reformers and, shortly before being ordained as an archbishop, married the daughter of the German Reformer Andreas Osiander—a fact that he hid for many years. Yet Cranmer only plodded along in his development as a Reformer, and he was willing to tarry for the sake of his king, who disliked Luther and held traditional religious views.

Nevertheless, by the king's authority, Cranmer led the English church away from its allegiance to Rome and championed the king's headship over the church. During the following decade, he faithfully served his king amid the flux of religious politics and a string of Henry's new wives. The king would ultimately have 6 wives, who gave him three children: Mary, the daughter of Catherine of Aragon; Elizabeth, the daughter of Anne Boleyn; and, finally, a son and heir to the throne, Edward, whose mother Jane Seymour died soon after childbirth.

As Henry lay dying in 1547, Cranmer was at his side. And during the reign of Henry's son, Cranmer was able to pursue reform of the English church more eagerly. Having been tutored by evangelicals, Edward VI, who came to the throne at the early age of 9, was compared to the biblical king Josiah. English Protestants hoped he would purge the land of what they saw as popish idolatry. Indeed, during this period, England became a home to Protestant refugees from continental Europe, including the famous Reformer Martin Bucer of Strasbourg. During Edward's reign, Cranmer also produced his most lasting work: the 1549 English *Book of Common Prayer* (quoted above), followed by a significant revision in 1552.[3]

But Protestant hopes for England would collapse suddenly in 1553, when the young king became ill and died. Four days later, through the working of Edward's council, a new monarch was named—and not one of Henry's children. Rather, the 15-year-old Lady Jane Grey reluctantly accepted the crown, urged to do so by the council and by her family.

But Jane's reign lasted only nine days. King Henry VIII's first daughter, Mary Tudor, paraded into England and was popularly proclaimed the rightful queen. Tragically, many of the ambitious men who compelled Jane to take the crown abandoned her—including her own father. And, though she gladly surrendered the crown to Mary, she couldn't save her life. After bravely defending her evangelical beliefs, she was beheaded on the morning of Feb. 12, 1554.[4]

A devout Catholic, Queen Mary desired to restore the pope's authority in England and to expel the Protestant faith from the land. During her reign, 280 men and women accused of the Protestant heresy were burned alive at the stake—earning for the queen the name, "Bloody Mary." And the English Protestant most despised by the queen was Cranmer, whom she begrudged for putting her mother to shame and for dissolving the church's allegiance to Rome.

So authorities, after imprisoning Cranmer and condemning him to death, bent all their efforts to break his resolve and make him recant his evangelical faith. Indeed, he did recant and was forced to sign several documents stating his recantation. But even this wouldn't save his life.

Then, on the night of March 17, he had his dream. He saw the kings, Henry VIII and Jesus Christ, and both kings rejected him. "Cranmer, shut off from both life and afterlife, could turn only to the mouth of hell," historian Diarmaid MacCulloch writes in his superb biography of Cranmer. "There could be no more eloquent parable or expression of his torment."[5]

Although Cranmer would sign another lengthy recantation the following morning, a war still raged for his eternal welfare. More visibly, this war, as MacCulloch writes, was "waged among his own flesh and blood, between his two sisters"—one Catholic and one Protestant.[6]

After enduring much emotional turmoil, something changed in Cranmer's demeanor on March 20, his last full day to live. This day, MacCulloch says, was "oddly tranquil." The following day, before facing the flames, Cranmer made a public confession of his faith. But he didn't confess his renewed faith in the Roman church, as his captors expected.[7]

"And now I come to the great thing, which so much troubleth my conscience, more than any thing that ever I did or said in my whole life, and that is the setting abroad of a writing contrary to the truth," he declared. And with these words, he denounced all he had penned against the Protestant faith since his imprisonment, having written them "contrary to the truth which I thought in my heart, and written for fear of death, and to save my life if it might be."

"And," he said, "forasmuch, as my hand offended, writing contrary to my heart, my hand shall first be punished."[8]

Soon, Cranmer was pulled down from his pulpit and led to the fire. He was fastened to the stake with an iron chain and, after the wood was set aflame, he fulfilled his promise.

"Stretching out his arm," the martyrologist John Foxe writes, "he put his right hand into the flame. ... And using often the words of Stephen, 'Lord Jesus, receive my spirit,' in the greatness of the flame, he gave up the ghost."[9]

> *"And, forasmuch, as my hand offended, writing contrary to my heart, my hand shall first be punished."*
>
> -Thomas Cranmer

19.

'REFORMATION WITHOUT TARRYING FOR ANY'

When King Henry VIII's Catholic daughter, Mary Tudor, claimed the throne of England in 1553, the English Reformer John Hooper backed her claim as legitimate. Since Hooper was staunchly Protestant bishop, his support of the new Catholic queen may come as a surprise. What comes as less of a surprise is his opposition to other leading Protestants in England, who aimed to prevent Mary from taking up the throne of England. This wasn't the first time that he bucked the views of his ecclesiastical superiors.[1]

Earlier, during the reign of the Protestant King Edward VI, Hooper stood against Archbishop Thomas Cranmer and other clergymen by refusing to wear a liturgical garment called a surplice during worship services. To modern-day readers, the dispute may seem trivial—a mere matter of clothes. But at the heart of this debate lay a fundamental question about the extent and nature of the Reformation in England.

Hooper's debate with his fellow Protestant clergymen pointed out two different views about the authority of Scripture as it relates to the church: On the one hand, Hooper's opponents in this debate insisted that any practice not prohibited by Scripture can be enforced for the sake of good order and unity within the church. In other words, unless the Bible says something is off-limits, it is generally permissible. The Bible doesn't prohibit clergymen from wearing special vestments during worship; therefore, the church can require them to do so. More recently, this first view has been labelled the "normative principle."[2]

But, on the contrary, Hooper insisted that the church should practice only what the Bible explicitly commands. Of course, he believed that anything the Bible prohibits is sinful. But he also said that the church can't enforce a practice unless it is a biblical mandate. Therefore, the church can't force him to wear the surplice during worship. This second view has been dubbed the "regulative principle."[3]

After facing a short time in prison for his views, Hooper submitted to the church—perhaps concluding that "vestments were not worth dying for." Yet only a few years later, during the reign of Queen Mary I, he was burned at the stake for his beliefs, alongside some of the fellow Protestants he had previously opposed. Nevertheless, the questions their debate had raised about the Bible's authority and the extent of the Reformation foreshadowed religious tensions of the next reign.

When Queen Mary died childless in 1558, she was succeeded by her half-sister, the daughter of Anne Boleyn and Henry VIII—namely, Queen Elizabeth I. Soon after coming to power, the new queen restored a Protestant settlement in England. Parliament declared that she was the "Supreme Governor" of the church in England and that the church's worship would be based on Thomas Cranmer's 1552 *Book of Common Prayer*, though with a few significant changes: For example, one revision made the prayer book more ambiguous, allowing it to support different views on the Lord's Supper.

As has often been noted by historians, Elizabeth cared little about opening "windows into men's souls." She didn't pry into people's personal beliefs, but she did demand outward conformity and unity in public worship.

But some Protestants, having spent the previous reign in exile among "Calvinists" in Geneva and other European cities, returned to England fully convinced of the same "regulative principle" that Hooper had defended. Others, having remained in England during the previous reign, slowly realized that—despite persecution—the church could exist without the monarch's permission. And many of them believed Elizabeth's religious settlement fell short of endorsing the biblical model of the church.

These "Puritans"—a name given to this diverse group by their opponents—called for greater biblical purity and reform in the church. Some of them, in fact, absolutely refused to settle for Elizabeth's religious settlement. Instead, they separated from the national church; hence, they've been dubbed "separatists." As the separatist Robert Browne wrote, they demanded a "reformation without tarrying for any."

As the following chapters will show, these Puritan and separatist strains in English Protestantism would have a deep impact on English-speaking Christianity for centuries.

> "Men's religion to God is between God and themselves. The king shall not answer for it. Neither may the King be judge between God and man. Let them be heretic, Turks, Jews, or whatsoever, it appertains not to the earthly power to punish them in the least measure."
>
> -Thomas Helwys

20.

A RELIGION OF THE BOOK: THE KING JAMES BIBLE

When Queen Elizabeth I died childless after 45 years in power, the dynasty of the Tudor family descended from Henry VIII also ended. Now, the English monarchy went to the Stuart family and, specifically, to the Scottish King James VI—now crowned also as King James I of England.

During his reign in Scotland, King James became familiar with the Calvinist Christianity that had led to Puritanism in England, since the Scottish church took steps toward reform in 1560 and laid the foundations for modern-day Presbyterianism. The king disliked and lobbied against the Presbyterian form of church government formulated in Calvin's Geneva. He suspected that, just as Geneva had overthrown its rulers and established a republic, even so Scottish Presbyterians would prefer an egalitarian republic above a monarchy. "No bishops, no king," he famously quipped, supporting the rule of a hierarchy of bishops over the church.[1]

The new king also disliked the Geneva Bible, a translation of Scripture preferred by English Puritans and separatists. First published in 1560, this translation was used by Shakespeare and was carried across the sea to Plymouth rock by the Pilgrims. One need not search long to find the reason for King James's aversion to the translation, since its marginal notes often opposed tyranny. Summarizing these notes, historian Alistair McGrath writes, "Tyrannical kings should not be obeyed; indeed, there were excellent reasons for suggesting that they should be overthrown." King James saw the threatening nature of these notes, and—as chapter 22 will make clear—his own son later discovered how grave these threats were.

So, from the beginning of his reign in England, the new king was suspicious of his Puritan subjects. Nevertheless, when he traveled to England to accept his crown, the Puritans remained hopeful that he would endorse further reform in England. They had reason to hope, since the king's realm of Scotland had advanced the Reformation cause more than England had; however, as already mentioned, they misread the situation.

Still, they approached the king even as he traveled to London in 1603, presenting him with a "Millenary Petition," signed by 1,000 ministers and urging him to reform the church. The king largely denied their requests. But when the Puritan leader John Reynolds later proposed a new English translation of the Bible, the king agreed to the request. Perhaps he thought this would appease some Puritans, who disliked the current authorized translation called the Bishop's Bible, while also replacing the Geneva Bible with its threatening notes.

When translation committees gathered to begin their work, they were directed to use earlier English translations if they agreed with the original Greek and Hebrew texts of the Bible. These included the Bishop's Bible, the Geneva Bible, Whitchurch's, Coverdale's, Matthew's and—at the foundation of all of them—William Tyndale's translation.[3]

As a result of the committees' efforts, the Authorized or King James Version (KJV) of the Bible was published in 1611, and it would stand alone as the premiere English translation until the 20th century. Through this translation, English Christianity became a "religion of the book."[4] By the 19th century, the words of the KJV were on the tongues of Anglicans, Catholics, Baptists and atheists alike. English-speaking children learned to read from this translation. Writing about 19th-century Bible reading in England, historian Timothy Larsen illustrates this point:

> *"Catherine Mumford (1829-1890) became well known as the co-founder of the Salvation Army under her married name of Catherine Booth. She was raised as an earnest evangelical Methodist. Not from a socially elite family, her father was a coach builder. Catherine did not receive any formal schooling until she had reached the age of twelve, and then, it was all over within two years. Her home schooling, however, was centered on the Bible. She was already reading it by the age of five. Before she reached the age of twelve and was sent off to school, she had 'read the sacred Book from cover to cover eight times through.'"*[5]

The "sacred Book" that Mumford read was the KJV.

Finally, although some modern-day readers find the KJV's older form of English difficult to read, the translation actually has a simple, yet graceful, style. This is made clear by comparing it with Edward Harwood's 18th-century attempt to provide an eloquent translation, consistent with the literary fashions of his time.[6] Consider the following example:

- The KJV, in Luke 15:11-12, reads, "A certain man had two sons: And the younger of them said to his father, 'Father, give me the portion of goods that falleth to me.' And he divided unto them his living."

- Harwood's translation of the same passage reads, "A Gentleman of a splendid family and opulent fortune had two sons. One day the younger approached his father, and begged him in the most importunate and soothing terms to make a partition of his effects betwixt himself and his elder brother—The indulgent father, overcome by his blandishments, immediately divided all his fortunes betwixt them."

Consider also 1 Corinthians 13:4-7:

- The KJV reads, "Charity suffereth long, and is kind; charity envieth not; charity vaunteth not itself, is not puffed up, Doth not behave itself unseemly, seeketh not her own, is not easily provoked, thinketh no evil; Rejoiceth not in iniquity, but rejoiceth in the truth; Beareth all things, believeth all things, hopeth all things, endureth all things."

- Harwood's translation reads, "Benevolence is unruffled; is benign: Benevolence cherishes no ambitious desires: Benevolence is not ostentatious; is not inflated with insolence. It preserves a consistent decorum; is not enslaved to sordid interest; is not transported with furious passion; indulges no malevolent design. It conceives no delight from the perpetration of wickedness; but is first to applaud truth and virtue. It throws a vail of candour over all things: is disposed to believe all things: views all things in the most favourable light: supports all things with serene composure."

In short, we're fortunate that the KJV, rather than Harwood's translation, endured to influence modern English Bible translations.

21.

BAPTISTS, PILGRIMS, AND THE CRY FOR FREEDOM

In 1612, eight years before the Pilgrims set sail for the New World to find a home where they could worship together in freedom, Baptist pastor Thomas Helwys proclaimed a message that would transform Western civilization for centuries to come.

Writing to King James I, Helwys published a tract called *A Short Declaration of the Mistery of Iniquity*, and in it he wrote the following inscription: "Hear, O king, and despise not the counsel of the poor, and let their complaints come before thee. The king is a mortal man and not God, therefore has no power over the immortal souls of his subjects, to make laws and ordinances for them, and to set spiritual lords over them. If the king has authority to make spiritual lords and laws, then he is an immortal God and not a mortal man."

He added, "Men's religion to God is between God and themselves. The king shall not answer for it. Neither may the King be judge between God and man. Let them be heretic, Turks, Jews, or whatsoever, it appertains not to the earthly power to punish them in the least measure."[1]

The year before he published these words, Helwys returned to England from the Netherlands with his congregation. They were the first Baptist church ever planted on English soil. And, despite the persecution they would face, they desired to bring the light of God's word back to their homeland.

The journey of the Baptist congregation began, in 1608, when Helwys and his followers fled persecution as part of a separatist congregation led by John Smyth.[2] This was the second separatist group from England to settle in Amsterdam, and for a short time Smyth's congregation dwelt peacefully alongside the congregation led by Francis Johnson. But in time a dispute broke out between the two churches about the biblical definition of church leadership.

This dispute exacerbated tensions within Smyth's own congregation. And, about 100 members led by John Robinson split from the church and moved to the city of Leiden. Eventually, Robinson's congregation set out from Plymouth, England, to the New World. These Pilgrims landed at Plymouth Rock in Massachusetts in 1620.[3]

Meanwhile, Smyth became convinced that infants are incapable of faith or repentance and, therefore, that they shouldn't be baptized. In 1609, he instituted believer's baptism within his church by baptizing himself and then the members of his congregation. In doing so, he established the first ever English Baptist church.

But Smyth's spiritual journey continued. Concerned that his self-baptism was inappropriate, Smyth joined the Dutch Waterlander Mennonites. The Englishmen and women who followed Smyth settled into an Amsterdam Bakehouse purchased from the Mennonites and eventually were integrated into Dutch society.[4]

But part of Smyth's congregation, led by Helwys, returned to England to proclaim God's word. This church of "General Baptists"—so called because they believed in general atonement, in contrast to the Reformed doctrine of particular atonement—called the king to tolerate the various religious groups in England.

Established a few decades later, England's "Particular Baptist" churches—which were basically Reformed in their beliefs—likewise defended religious liberty. As stated in the 1689 London Baptist Confession of Faith, "God alone is Lord of the conscience, and hath left it free from the doctrines and commandments of men which are in anything contrary to his word, or not contained in it."[5]

Likewise, Baptists in the American colonies would carry on the tradition of defending religious liberty, becoming key proponents of this freedom as the Bill of Rights was drafted and approved by the fledgling United States of America. In 1773, Isaac Backus wrote, "Religious matters are to be separated from the jurisdiction of the state, not because they are beneath the interests of the state but, quite to the contrary, because they are too high and holy and thus are beyond the competence of the state."[6]

Similarly, in 1791, John Leland declared, "Every man must give an account of himself to God, and therefore every man ought to be at liberty to serve God in that way that he can best reconcile it to his conscience. If government can answer for individuals at the day of judgment, let men be controlled by it in religious matters; otherwise let men be free."[7]

> "Every man must give an account of himself to God, and therefore every man ought to be at liberty to serve God in that way that he can best reconcile it to his conscience. If government can answer for individuals at the day of judgment, let men be controlled by it in religious matters; otherwise let men be free."
>
> -John Leland

22.

REVOLUTION AND THE END OF THE REFORMATION AGE

> *"… till one shall rise,*
> *Of proud, ambitious heart, who, not content*
> *With fair equality, fraternal state,*
> *Will arrogate dominion undeserved*
> *Over his brethren…."*
>
> – *John Milton*, **Paradise Lost** *(Book 12, lines 24-28)*[1]

The great 17th-century poet John Milton published these words nearly two decades after King Charles I lost his head. In this passage from Milton's classic poem, *Paradise Lost*, the angel Michael speaks to the fallen father of the human race, Adam, foretelling the rise of tyranny on the earth. Inspired by the same pride and ambition that motivated Satan in Milton's epic, this tyranny brings men and women under the yolk of unjust "dominion."[2]

Accused of tyranny and suspected by English Protestants as being fond of Roman Catholicism, King Charles I—the son of King James I, who had authorized the publication of the King

James Bible—lost his crown and his life after a long conflict with Parliament. Once the king attempted to arrest members of Parliament, their conflict soon broke out into the English Civil War of 1642-1651.

At first, Protestants upheld a united front against the king, but their ranks began to break into disunity—especially as radical groups, like the "Fifth Monarchy" and the "Levellers," gained popularity in the army, where they predicted Christ's impending return and declared that society should be upturned and a radical equality enforced. Parliament resisted this message, and the army turned against the assembly, ultimately seizing control of the king and arresting 45 ministers of Parliament. In a "Rump Parliament" supported by the army and dominated by the House of Commons, King Charles I was accused of treason and beheaded on January 30, 1649.

Then, amid the resulting pandemonium, Oliver Cromwell—a devout Puritan and leader in Parliament—accepted and held power as Lord Protector of England until his death in 1658. He was succeeded by his son, Richard, who quickly abdicated from the protectorate. As a result, with nothing left to do, Parliament restored King Charles II—the son of the beheaded king—to the throne in 1660.

But, on his deathbed, the new king proclaimed his allegiance to the Catholic Church, and his son King James II likewise favored Catholicism. As a result, in the "Glorious Revolution" of 1688, the English people once again rebelled and called the Protestant Prince William of Orange and his wife, Mary, to rule as king and queen in England.[3]

This story of civil war and revolution had a significant impact for centuries to come, and it formed the backdrop for some of the most important religious leaders and writings to come out of 17th-century England—including, to begin with, Milton and his *Paradise Lost*:

- **John Milton (1608-1674)** is best known today as the poet who penned the classic, *Paradise Lost*, an epic recounting the fall of mankind into sin. Yet Milton opposed King Charles I during the English Civil War, and his political tracts were no less significant than his poetry. His *Areopagitica* of 1644 opposed censorship imposed by the government and is a classic defense of free speech. Moreover, through political tracts like the *Eikonoklastes* and *The Tenure of Kings and Magistrates* (both published in 1649), Milton would be among authors who inspired the colonists during the American Revolution a century later. "The colonists (during the American Revolution)," historian Bernard Bailyn once wrote, "identified themselves with these seventeenth-century heroes of liberty."[4]

- **John Bunyan (1628-1688)**, like Milton, left a literary heritage for English Christians, and he also played a role in events surrounding the English Civil War, having served with the Parliamentary army. Only after leaving the army and settling down with his wife was Bunyan spiritually reborn, and following his conversion he was baptized by the Baptist pastor John Gifford in 1655. He soon was a deacon and, later, a pastor and fearless preacher—being placed in prison for a 12-year period from 1660-1672 and returning to prison in 1676. In prison, he wrote the Christian classic, *The Pilgrim's Progress*—an allegory about each Christian's journey through life that formed the religious imaginations of generations to come.[5]

- **John Owen (1616-1683)**, a theologian and Congregationalist minister, was invited to preach before Parliament the day after the beheading of King Charles I. The 32-year-old Owen preached on Jeremiah 15:19-20. A later sermon based on Hebrew 12:27 brought him to the attention of soon-to-be Lord Protector Oliver

Cromwell, whose companionship he enjoyed for a time. In 1658, Owen also joined the assembly that created *The Savoy Declaration*—a revision of the Westminster Confession of Faith, which was itself written under the auspices of the Protestant Parliament in 1646 during the civil war. Owen is known today for his many theological writings, including works of practical theology like *The Mortification of Sin* and *Spiritual Mindedness*, as well as theological tomes on the Trinity, the Holy Spirit, and the work of Christ.[6]

Milton, Bunyan and Owen were heirs to a Reformation that began a century before their births. But their lives also overlapped with the lives of thinkers who established foundations for both the skepticism and the piety of another era—namely, the 18th-century age of Enlightenment. Such thinkers include men like Francis Bacon, John Locke, Rene Descartes, Blaise Pascal, Baruch Spinoza, Philip Jakob Spener and August Hermann Francke.

So it is that, during the lives of Milton, Bunyan and Owen, we finally come to the end of the Reformation era.

23

'WE ARE BEGGARS! THAT IS TRUE!'

Early in the year 1546, Martin Luther set out to his birthplace in Eisleben, Germany, to preach a series of sermons and ordain two new pastors. While urging his listeners to faith, he stopped his last sermon abruptly, saying he hadn't the strength to go on. He commented that much more deserved to be said, stepped down from the pulpit, and took a seat.

One of his aides during the service recounted how Luther murmured to himself after sitting down: "A Christian," he said, "is only certain about the devil when he believes that Christ is his wisdom, salvation, righteousness and redemption." As historian Martin Marty has noted, these words described the central Reformation truth that Luther had first proclaimed nearly three decades earlier. But "now he spoke urgently," wrestling once again with God, striving to maintain his own faith to the end.[1]

For decades Luther's health had been poor. In fact, as early as 1527, he had a near death experience that prompted his close friends to record his words as if they would be his last. But at that time, Luther regained his strength and continued to work feverishly for the reform of the church.[2] In 1546, however, Luther's health quickly declined, and he would not recover.

Yet Luther didn't fear death; instead, he strove to die in the faith that he preached throughout his life. As he lay dying, he reassured his wife, Katherine, with a tender affirmation of his trust in Christ—that majestic Lord over creation who humbled Himself to become a helpless infant.

"Free me from your worries," he told her. "I have a caretaker who is better than you and all the angels; he lies in the cradle and rests on a virgin's bosom, and yet, nevertheless, he sits at the right hand of God, the almighty Father."[3]

Then, on Feb. 16, 1546, he jotted down a note, reflecting human unworthiness before God and His Word.

"Let no one think he has sufficiently grasped the Holy Scriptures, unless he has governed the churches for a hundred years with prophets like Elijah and Elisha, John the Baptist, Christ, and the apostles. Don't venture on this divine *Aeneid*, but rather bend low in reverence before its footprints! We are beggars! That is true!"[4]

Two days after penning these words, Luther died.

"We are beggars! That is true!" Few phrases from Luther's pen could better help us as we struggle to understand and evaluate the Reformation that Luther ignited 29 years before his death. It is rightly said that each of the Reformers were beggars, and their achievements were accompanied by flaws. Yet they were beggars—bending low before Scripture, ready to submit to its truth, humbled by its laws, openhanded and eager to accept its gospel promises.

"We are beggars." This confession is implicit in the core

theological principles that have come down to us from the Reformation. We are saved by grace alone, through faith alone, in Christ alone. We have nothing that we can offer God, no good deed that can atone for our evil deeds or, more importantly, for the wickedness of our sinful hearts. Yet Christ alone has taken the penalty for our sins in his death and has conquered both sin and death through his resurrection. By placing our trust wholly in Him, we can find mercy and a new life in the Spirit. We are beggars all, but the Lord of Creation has deigned to care for all our needs.

This confession also teaches us how to respond when we find that the heroes of the Reformation sometimes fell short of the mark and displayed their fallibility. What do we do when we discover that Martin Luther, toward the end of his life, wrote hatefully against the Jews?[5] What do we do when we find that Huldrych Zwingli, John Calvin and many other leaders of the Reformation were complicit in the persecution and execution of people who simply refused to accept their theological beliefs? What do we do when we hear about a set of Anabaptists who, in 1534, took over the city of Münster, endorsed polygamy and identified the city as the "new Jerusalem"? Much could be said in answer to these questions, but it would be well to start by remembering Luther's confession: We must remember that Luther, Zwingli, Calvin—in fact, all the Reformers—were beggars, burdened with their own frailties and caught up in events much bigger than themselves, which they did not always fully understand.

"We are beggars!" This is true for us, as well. So we need to place our trust not in ourselves, but in Jesus Christ. And we need to "bend low in reverence before" Scripture, accepting with gratitude the spiritual sustenance, the spiritual treasure that God gives us through His Word. Like the Reformers, we are beggars, we are fallible and borne down by our own weaknesses. Yet God's Word is true, and it will stand forever.

> "*Let no one think he has sufficiently grasped the Holy Scriptures, unless he has governed the churches for a hundred years with prophets like Elijah and Elisha, John the Baptist, Christ, and the apostles. Don't venture on this divine <u>Aeneid</u>, but rather bend low in reverence before its footprints! We are beggars! That is true!*"
>
> -Martin Luther

NOTES

Chapter 1
1. For the view that Luther pasted, rather than nailing, the 95 Theses to the church door, see http://www.albertmohler.com/2016/04/25/thinking-in-public-andrew-pettegree.
2. Martin Luther, "The Ninety-Five Theses (1517)," in *Martin Luther's Basic Theological Writings* (2nd edition), Timothy F. Lull, ed. (Minneapolis: Augsburg Fortress, 2005), 40-46.
3. A.H. Newman, "The Reformation From a Baptist Point of View," accessed online at http://www.baptisttheology.org/baptisttheology/assets/file/thereformationfromabaptistpointofview.pdf. Originally published in *The Baptist Quarterly Review* 4 (1884).
4. Timothy George, *Theology of the Reformers*, Rev. Ed. (Nashville: B&H Academic, 2013), 55.

Chapter 2
1. G.K. Chesterton, "The Ballad of the White Horse," in *The Works of G.K. Chesterton* (Wordsworth Editions Ltd, 1995), 166.
2. Roland H. Bainton, *Here I Stand: A Life of Martin Luther* (Nashville: Abingdon Press, 1950), 15.
3. Heiko Oberman, *The Impact of the Reformation* (Grand Rapids: Eerdmans, 1994), 68.
4. C.S. Lewis, "De Descriptione Temporum," in *They Asked for a Paper: Papers and Addresses* (London: Geoffrey Bles, 1962), 10.
5. James R. Ginther, *The Westminster Handbook to Medieval Theology* (Louisville: Westminster John Knox Press, 2009), xi-xx.

Chapter 3
1. Thom Satterlee, "Burning Wyclif," in *Burning Wyclif: Poems* (Texas Tech University Press, 2006), 64.
2. Bainton, *Here I Stand*, 89.
3. Ibid.
4. Oberman, *Luther: Man Between God and the Devil* (New Haven: Yale University Press, 1982), 53-57.

5. G.W. Bernard, *The Late Medieval English Church: Vitality and Vulnerability before the Break with Rome* (New Haven: Yale University Press), 229; Margaret Aston, *Lollards and Reformers: Images and Literacy in Late Medieval Religion* (London: The Hambledon Press, 1984), 171-75.

6. Oberman, *Luther: Man Between God and the Devil*, 55.

Chapter 4

1. Francis Schaeffer, *How Should We Then Live? The Rise and Decline of Western Thought and Culture* (Old Tappan, N.J.: Revell, 1976).

2. James R. Payton, Jr. *Getting the Reformation Wrong: Correcting Some Misunderstandings* (Downers Grove: IVP Academic, 2010; kindle edition), loc. 498.

3. Steven Ozment, *The Serpent and the Lamb: Cranach, Luther and the Making of the Reformation* (New Haven: Yale University Press, 2011).

4. Desiderius Erasmus, "Paraclesis," in *Christian Humanism and the Reformation: Selected Writings of Erasmus*, ed. John C. Olin (New York: Fordham University Press, 1987), 101.

Chapter 5

1. Bainton, *Here I Stand*, 105-16.

2. Bernhard Lohse, *Martin Luther's Theology: Its Historical and Systematic Development* (Minneapolis: Fortress Press, 1999), 85-95.

3. *Luther's Works*, vol. 34 (Fortress Press, 1960), 336-37.

4. Martin Luther, "The Freedom of a Christian," in *Three Treatises* (Fortress Press, 1990), 261-316.

5. Ibid.

6. Ibid.

7. Ibid.

Chapter 6

1. Luther, "The Babylonian Captivity of the Church," *Three Treatises*, 113-260.

2. Cited by Paul Althaus, *The Ethics of Martin Luther* (Philadelphia: Fortress Press, 1965), 104.

3. Ibid.

Chapter 7
1. F.F. Bruce, *Romans*, in Tyndale New Testament Commentaries (Grand Rapids: Eerdmans, 1985), 38.
2. Bainton, *Here I Stand*, 129-48.

Chapter 8
1. Bainton, *Here I Stand*, 159.

Chapter 9
1. Stephen Reed Cattley, ed., *The Acts and Monuments of John Foxe: A New and Complete Edition*, vol. 5 (London: R. B. Seeley and W. Burnside, 1838), 3.
2. John Frith, "The Articles Wherefore John Frith Died," in *The Works of John Frith*, The Courtenay Library of Reformation Classics, ed. N.T. Wright (Oxford: The Sutton Courtenay Press, 1978), 450-56.
3. Carl R. Trueman, *Luther's Legacy: Salvation and English Reformers, 1535-1556* (Oxford: Clarendon Press, 1994), 121-55.
4. Wayne Grudem, *Systematic Theology: An Introduction to Biblical Doctrine* (Grand Rapids: Zondervan, 1994), 994.

Chapter 10
1. Thomas Müntzer, "Sermon before the Princes," in *Spiritual and Anabaptist Writers*, ed. G. H. Williams and Angle M. Mergal, vol. 25 of the Library of Christian Classics (Philadelphia: Westminster Press, 1957), 63-68.
2. George Huntston Williams, *The Radical Reformation*, 3rd ed. (Kirksville: Truman State University Press, 2000), 133-34.
3. William R. Estep, *Renaissance and Reformation* (Grand Rapids: Eerdmans, 1986), 143.
4. Ibid., 146-47. Also, see Martin Luther, "Against the Robbing and Murdering Hordes of Peasants, May 1525," in *Martin Luther*, ed. E.G. Rupp and Benjamin Drewery (New York: St. Martin's Press, 1970), 125-26.
5. Grebel's letters to Müntzer, available online at www.anabaptistnetwork.com/grebel.
6. Harold Bender, "The Anabaptist Vision," *Church History* 13, no. 1 (1944): 14.
7. Letter available at www.anabaptistnetwork.com/grebel.

Chapter 11

1. William R. Estep, *The Anabaptist Story: An Introduction to Sixteenth-Century Anabaptism*, 3rd ed. (Grand Rapids: Eerdmans, 1996), 77.

2. Ibid., 93-94.

3. Ibid., 80.

4. Ibid., 79.

5. Balthasar Hubmaier, "On the Christian Baptism of Believers," in *Balthasar Hubmaier: Theologian of Anabaptism*, trans. and eds., H. Wayne Pipkin and John H. Yoder (Scottdale, PA: Herald Press, 1989), 127.

6. Hubmaier, "On Heretics and Those Who Burn Them," in *Balthasar Hubmaier: Theologian of Anabaptism*, 58-66.

7. Hubmaier, "Apologia," in *Balthasar Hubmaier: Theologian of Anabaptism*, 556-57.

Chapter 12

1. Estep, *The Anabaptist Story*, 267-306.

2. Kenneth R. Davis, "No Discipline, No Church: An Anabaptist Contribution to the Reformed Tradition," *SCJ* 13 (1982), 43-48; and also Malcolm B. Yarnell III, *The Formation of Christian Doctrine* (Nashville: B&H Academic, 2007), 92.

3. See Malcolm B. Yarnell III, ed., *The Anabaptists and Contemporary Baptists: Restoring New Testament Christianity, Essays in Honor of Paige Patterson* (Nashville: B&H Academic, 2013); cf. Anthony L. Chute, Nathan A. Finn and Michael A.G. Haykin, *The Baptist Story: From English Sect to Global Movement* (Nashville: B&H Academic, 2015), 11-38, and James Leo Garrett, *Baptist Theology: A Four-Century Study* (Macon, GA: Mercer University Press, 2009), 8-15.

Chapter 13

1. Estep, *Renaissance and Reformation*, 235.

2. Ibid.

3. See John C. Olin, ed., *A Reformation Debate: Sadoleto's Letter to the Genevans and Calvin's Reply* (New York: Harper & Row, 1966), 60.

4. Ibid., 61.

5. Dawn DeVries, "Calvin's preaching," in *The Cambridge Companion to John Calvin*, ed. Donald M. McKim (Cambridge: University Press, 2004), 111.

6. John Calvin, *Institutes of the Christian Religion*, vol 1, ed. John T. McNeil (Louisville: Westminster John Knox Press, 1960), 6-8.

7. Ibid., 70.

Chapter 14

1. Carl R. Trueman, "Calvin and Calvinism," in *The Cambridge Companion to John Calvin*, 225-44.

2. Richard A. Muller, "Was Calvin a Calvinist? Or, Did Calvin (or Anyone Else in the Early Modern Era) Plant the 'TULIP'?", 5. Accessed online [27 July 2017]: https://www.calvin.edu/meeter/Was%20Calvin%20a%20Calvinist-12-26-09.pdf.

3. See, for example, Kevin Kennedy, *Union with Christ and the Extent of the Atonement in Calvin* (New York: Peter Lang, 2002).

4. Trueman, "Calvin and Calvinism," 225-44; Muller, "Was Calvin a Calvinist?", 16.

5. Heidelberg Catechism available online at: www.ligonier.org/learn/articles/heidelberg-catechism-1563/.

Chapter 15

1. Carter Lindberg, *The European Reformations* (Malden, Mass.: Blackwell Publishers, 1996), 335-56.

2. Estep, *Renaissance and Reformation*, 271-72.

3. Lindberg, *The European Reformations*, 345-50.

4. Estep, *Renaissance and Reformation*, 277.

Chapter 16

1. William Tyndale, "An Answer to Sir Thomas More's Dialogue," in *An Answer to Sir Thomas More's Dialogue, The Supper of the Lord after the Meaning of John VI and 1 Cor. XI., and WM. Tracy's Testament Expounded*, ed., Henry Walter (Cambridge: University Press, 1850), 185.

2. Diarmaid MacCulloch, *The Reformation: A History* (New York: Penguin, 2005), 88.

3. "The Council of Trent," in *Readings in Christian Thought*, 2nd ed., ed. Hugh T. Kerr (Nashville: Abingdon Press, 1996), 175-79.

4. Ibid.

5. Ibid.

6. Ibid.

7. Carter, *The European Reformations*, 356.

Chapter 17

1. John Guy, *Tudor England* (Oxford: University Press, 1988), 1.

2. See J.J. Scarisbrick, *Henry VIII* (Berkeley: University of California Press, 1968); G.W. Bernard, *The King's Reformation: Henry VIII and the Remaking of the English Church* (New Haven: Yale University Press, 2005).

3. Cattley, ed., *Acts and Monuments* (by John Foxe), 117.

4. See Peter Ackroyd, *The Life of Thomas More* (New York: Anchor Books, 1998); and Brian Moynahan, *God's Bestseller: William Tyndale, Thomas More, and the Writing the English Bible—A Story of Martyrdom and Betrayal* (New York: St. Martin's Press, 2014).

5. E.G. Rupp, *Studies in the Making of the English Protestant Tradition (Mainly in the Reign of Henry VIII)* (Cambridge: University Press, 1949), 128-29.

Chapter 18

1. Robert Van de Weyer, *First English Prayer Book: The First Worship Edition Since the Original Publication in 1549* (Circle Books, 2008).

2. Diarmaid MacCulloch, *Thomas Cranmer: A Life* (New Haven: Yale University Press, 1996), 598.

3. MacCulloch, in ibid., recounts Cranmer's achievements.

4. A helpful article on Lady Jane Grey can be accessed online at https://blogs.thegospelcoalition.org/justintaylor/2014/02/12/the-execution-of-lady-jane-grey-460-years-ago-today/.

5. MacCulloch, *Thomas Cranmer*, 598.

6. Ibid., 605.

7. Ibid., 599-605.

8. W. Grinton Berry, *Foxe's Book of Martyrs* (Spire, 1998), 351-87.

9. Ibid.

Chapter 19
1. Trueman, *Luther's Legacy*, 27-30.
2. Gregg R. Allison, *Historical Theology: An Introduction to Christian Doctrine* (Zondervan, 2011; Kindle edition), 659-733.
3. Ibid.
4. Trueman, *Luther's Legacy*, 27.

Chapter 20
1. Alistair E. McGrath, *In the Beginning: The Story of the King James Bible and How it Changed a Nation, a Language, and a Culture* (New York: Anchor Books, 2002), 130-48.
2. Ibid., 144.
3. Ibid., 130-71; 67-98.
4. Timothy T. Larsen, "Literacy and Biblical Knowledge: The Victorian Age and Our Own," *JETS* 52/3 (2009), 520.
5. See David Daniell, *The Bible in English: Its History and Influence* (New Haven: Yale University Press, 2003), 604-623.

Chapter 21
1. Chute, Finn and Haykin, *The Baptist Story*, 19-20.
2. Ibid., 14-20.
3. A brief analysis of this Baptist-Pilgrim connection is available online at http://www.bpnews.net/43822/pilgrims-and-baptists-the-little-known-connection.
4. Keith Sprunger and Mary Sprunger, "The Church in the Bakehouse: John Smyth's English Anabaptist Congregation at Amsterdam, 1609-1660," *Mennonite Quarterly Review* 85 (2011), 219-58.
5. Available online at http://www.vor.org/truth/1689/1689bc00.html.
6. Joe Carter, "20 quotes from Baptists on religious liberty": http://erlc.com/resource-library/articles/20-quotes-from-baptists-on-religious-liberty.
7. Ibid.; see also R. Stanton Norman, *The Baptist Way: Distinctives of a Baptist Church* (Nashville: B&H Academic), 157-83.

Chapter 22

1. Laurence Lerner, ed., *The English Poems of John Milton* (Wordsworth Poetry Library, 2004), 397.

2. Ibid.; see also C.S. Lewis, *A Preface to Paradise Lost* (Oxford: University Press, 1969), 78.

3. Justo L. González, *The Story of Christianity: vol. 2, The Reformation to the Present Day* (HarperSanFrancisco, 1985), 149-63.

4. Bernard Bailyn, *The Ideological Origins of the American Revolution* (Cambridge, Mass.: Harvard University Press, 1992), 34-35.

5. Bunyan left an account of his own life in "Grace Abounding to the Chief of Sinners: Or, A Brief Relation of the Exceeding Mercy of God in Christ, to His Poor Servant John Bunyan," in *Grace Abounding with Other Spiritual Autobiographies*, ed. John Stachniewski and Anita Pacheco, 1-94 (Oxford: Oxford University Press, 1998).

6. Sinclair B. Ferguson, "Profiles in Faith: John Owen (1616-1683)" (C.S. Lewis Institute, online): http://www.cslewisinstitute.org/webfm_send/611.

Chapter 23

1. Martin Marty, *Martin Luther: A Penguin Life* (New York: Viking/Penguin, 2004), 182-83.

2. Oberman, *Luther: Man between God and the Devil*, 320-24.

3. Marty, *Martin Luther*, 185.

4. Ibid.

5. On Luther and the Jews, see Carl R. Trueman, *Histories and Fallacies: Problems Faced in the Writing of History* (Wheaton, Ill.: Crossway, 2010), 129-38.

FURTHER READING

General Histories of the Reformation
Janz, Denis R., ed. *A Reformation Reader: Primary Texts with Introductions*. Minneapolis: Fortress Press, 2008.

Bainton, Roland H. *The Reformation of the Sixteenth Century*. rev. and enl. ed. Boston: Beacon Press, 1985.

George, Timothy. *Theology of the Reformers*. Nashville, TN: Broadman Press, 1988.

Lindberg, Carter, ed. *The Reformation Theologians*. Malden, MA: Blackwell, 2002.

MacCulloch, Diarmaid. *The Reformation: A History*. New York: Viking, 2003.

Ozment, Steven. *The Age of Reform, 1250-1550*. New Haven: Yale University Press, 1980.

Payton, James R., Jr. *Getting the Reformation Wrong: Correcting Some Misunderstandings*. Downers Grove, Ill.: IVP Academic, 2010.

Premature Reformation/Humanism
Bainton, Roland. *Erasmus of Christendom*. New York: Scribner, 1969.

Evans, G. R. *John Wyclif: Myth and Reality*. Oxford: Lion, 2005.

Lambert, Malcolm. *Medieval Heresy: Popular Movements from the Gregorian Reform to the Reformation*. 3rd ed. Malden, MA: Blackwell, 2002.

McFarlane, K.B. *John Wycliffe and the Beginnings of English Nonconformity*. London: English Universities Press, 1952.

Spinka, Matthew. *John Huss: A Biography*. Westport, CT: Greenwood, 1968.

Martin Luther & Lutheranism
Althaus, Paul. *The Theology of Martin Luther*. Translated by Robert C. Schultz. Philadelphia: Fortress Press, 1966.

_____. *The Ethics of Martin Luther*, translated by Robert C. Schultz. Philadelphia: Fortress Press, 1972.

Bainton, Roland. *Here I Stand*. Reprinted edition. New York: Meridian- Penguin Books, 1995.

Lohse, Bernhard. *Martin Luther's Theology*. Translated by Roy Harrisville. Minneapolis: Fortress, 1999.

Lull, Timothy ed. *Martin Luther's Basic Theological Writings*. Minneapolis: Fortress, 2005.

Marty, Martin. *Martin Luther*. New York: Viking/Penguin, 2004.

Oberman, Heiko A. *Luther: Man Between God and the Devil*, Translated by Eileen Walliser-Schwarzbart. New York: Image-Doubleday, 1992.

The Reformed Tradition

Calvin, John. *Institutes of the Christian Religion*. 2 vols. Edited by John T. McNeill. Translated and annotated by Ford L. Battles. Library of Christian Classics Series nos. 20–21. London: SCM. Press, 1960.

_____. and Jacopo Sadoleto. *A Reformation Debate: Sadoleto's Letter to the Genevans and Calvin's Reply, with an Appendix on the Justification Controversy*. Edited with introduction by John C. Olin. Harper Torchbooks. New York: Harper and Row Publishers, 1966.

Benedict, Philip. *Christ's Churches Purely Reformed: A Social History of Calvinism*. New Haven: Yale University Press, 2002.

McKim, Daniel K, ed. *The Cambridge Companion to John Calvin*. Cambridge: Cambridge University Press, 2004.

Parker, T. H. L. *John Calvin: A Biography*. London: J. M. Dent and Sons, 1975.

Stephens, W. Peter. *Zwingli: An Introduction to His Thought*. New York: Oxford University Press, 1992.

Zwingli, Huldrych. "On the Certainty and Clarity of the Word of God." In *Zwingli and Bullinger: The Library of Christian Classics*. Philadelphia: Westminster Press, 1979.

The Radical Reformation

Estep, William Roscoe ed. *Anabaptist Beginnings (1523-1533): A Source Book*. Nieuwkoop: B. de Graaf, 1976.

Goertz, Hans-Jurgen, Ed. *Profiles of Radical Reformers*. Scottdale, PA: Herald Press, 1982.

Hubmaier, Balthasar. *Balthasar Hubmaier, Theologian of Anabaptism*. Translated and Edited by H. Wayne Pipkin and John Howard Yoder. Classics of the Radical Reformation, 5. Scottdale, PA: Herald Press, 1989.

Estep, William Roscoe. *The Anabaptist Story: An Introduction to Sixteenth-Century Anabaptism*. 2nd ed. Grand Rapids, MI: William B. Eerdmans Pub, 1996.

Snyder, C. Arnold. *Anabaptist History and Theology*. Kitchener, Ontario: Pandora Press, 1997.

Williams, George Huntston. *The Radical Reformation*. 3rd ed. Sixteenth Century Essays & Studies, Vol. 15. Kirksville, MO: Truman State University Press, 2000.

The English Reformation

Daniell, David. *William Tyndale: A Biography*. New Haven: Yale University Press, 1994.

Dickens, A.G. *The English Reformation*. New York: Schocken Books, 1964.

Lee, Jason K. *The Theology of John Smyth*. Macon: Mercer University Press, 2003.

MacCulloch, Diarmaid. *Thomas Cranmer: A Life*. New Haven, CT: Yale University Press, 1996.

Marshall, Peter. *Reformation England: 1480-1642*. New York: Bloomsbury Academic, 2012.

Trueman, Carl R. *Luther's Legacy: Salvation and English Reformers, 1525-1556*. Oxford: Clarendon Press, 1994.

Tyndale, William. *The Obedience of a Christian Man*. Edited and with and Introduction and notes by David Daniell. Penguin Classics. London: Penguin Books, 2000.

White, B. R. *The English Separatist Tradition: from the Marian Martyrs to the Pilgrim Fathers*. Oxford Theological Monographs. London: Oxford University Press, 1971.

Catholic Renewal/Counter-Reformation

Caraman, Philip. *Ignatius of Loyola: a Biography*. Chicago: Loyola University Press, 1990.

Council of Trent, and Henry Joseph Schroeder. *Canons and Decrees of the Council of Trent*. Rockford, Ill: Tan Books and Publishers, 1978.

Ignatius, of Loyola Saint. *Ignatius of Loyola: The Spiritual Exercises and Selected Works*. Edited by George E. Ganss. The Classics of Western spirituality. New York: Paulist Press, 1991.

Olin, John C. ed. *Catholic Reform from Cardinal Ximenes to the Council of Trent*. New York: Fordham University Press, 1990.

O'Malley, John. *Trent and All That: Renaming Catholicism in the Early Modern Era*. Cambridge, MA: Harvard University Press, 2000.